SPURGEON'S PRAYERS

SPURGEON'S PRAYERS

CHRISTIAN FOCUS PUBLICATIONS

ISBN 1 85792 041 4

This edition published in 1993
by
Christian Focus Publications Ltd
Geanies House, Fearn, Ross-shire,
IV20 1TW, Scotland, Great Britain.

Printed and Bound in Great Britain
by
Cox & Wyman Ltd., Reading, Berkshire

Cover design
by
Donna Macleod

Contents

INTRODUCTORY NOTE 9

LECTURE

THE GOLDEN KEY OF PRAYER 13

PRAYERS

PRAYER 1
Help from on High 37

PRAYER 2
Thanks be unto God 42

PRAYER 3
The Love without Measure or End 47

PRAYER 4
The All-prevailing Plea 52

PRAYER 5
To the King Eternal 57

PRAYER 6
The Wonders of Calvary...63

PRAYER 7
'Let all the people praise thee' 67

PRAYER 8
A Prayer for Holiness 71

PRAYER 9
Glorious Liberty 75

PRAYER 10
The Music of Praise 78

PRAYER 11
Under the Blood 82

PRAYER 12
On Holy Ground 87

PRAYER 13
The Wings of Prayer 91

PRAYER 14
'Bless the Lord, O my soul!' 95

PRAYER 15
The Peace of God 99

PRAYER 16
He ever liveth 103

PRAYER 17
To be like Christ 107

PRAYER 18
O, for more grace! 111

PRAYER 19
God's unspeakable gift 115

PRAYER 20
The Great Sacrifice 119

PRAYER 21
Boldness at the throne of grace 124

PRAYER 22
The presence of God 128

PRAYER 23
The Look of Faith 134

PRAYER 24
'Deliver us from evil' 137

PRAYER 25
The washing of water by the word 141

PRAYER 26
Prayer answered and unanswered 146

PRAYER MEETINGS -
AS THEY WERE AND AS THEY SHOULD BE........ 151

C. H. Spurgeon's Hymn for an early morning prayer meeting

Sweetly the holy hymn
Breaks on the morning air;
Before the world with smoke is dim
We meet to offer prayer.

While flowers are wet with dews,
Dew of our souls descend;
Ere yet the sun the day renews;
O Lord, Thy Spirit send!

Upon the battle field
Before the fight begins,
We seek, O Lord,
Thy sheltering shield,
To guard us from our sins!

Ere yet our vessel sails
Upon the stream of day
We plead, O Lord, for heavenly gales
To speed us on our way!

On the lone mountain side,
Before the morning's light,
The Man of Sorrows wept and cried,
And rose refresh'd with might.

Oh, hear us then, for we
Are very weak and frail!
We make the Saviour's Name our plea,
And surely must prevail.

INTRODUCTORY NOTE

Decidedly this selection of the great preacher's prayers supplies a want. Many of us have long hoped for such a volume; and now we welcome it with warm gratitude. It was memorable to hear this incomparable divine when he preached. It was often even more memorable to hear him pray.

Who talked with God as Spurgeon did? How naturally prayer fell from the lips of that great apostle! We felt that he was only doing before the multitude what he was habituated to do in private. Prayer was the instinct of his soul, and the atmosphere of his life. It was his 'vital breath' and 'native air'. How naturally he inhaled and exhaled it! He sped as on eagle's wings, into the heaven of God.

His wonderful knowledge of Scripture made his prayers fresh and edifying. No man can pray with high effect unless he is steeped in Scripture. Mr Spurgeon lived and moved and had his being in the Word of God. He knew its remoter reaches, its nooks and crannies. Its spirit had entered into his spirit; and when he prayed, the Spirit of God brought all manner of precious oracles to his mind.

Then he lived so entirely in the spiritual world that he was ever ready to pray. He had not to school himself at the moment. His pulpit-prayers were not art, but nature. Every prayer was the effluence of a consecrated personality. No liturgy could have restrained him. One could not imagine him making literary preparation for public prayer. The flower gave out its perfume without effort. The urn was ever being filled where the pure waters rise, and so afforded at any moment abundant refreshment.

The quivering sympathy of Mr Spurgeon's prayers thrilled all who heard them. You felt the throbbing of that mighty heart. He was royal in his tenderness. Whom did he forget in those powerful pleadings? The faith of this great saint indeed worked by love. His prayers grandly evinced this.

We covet for this volume a great constituency. Of a truth these prayers are ideals of how men ought to pray. They are calculated to be great inspirations to ministers as they contemplate their congregational prayers. To all Christian workers they will afford real enrichment. For quiet home reading they will be invaluable.

D T Y

Lecture

THE GOLDEN KEY OF PRAYER

THE GOLDEN KEY OF PRAYER

'Call unto Me, and I will answer thee, and shew thee great and mighty things, which thou knowest not' (Jeremiah 33:3).

Some of the most learned works in the world smell of the midnight oil; but the most spiritual and most comforting books and sayings of men usually have a savour about them of prison-damp. I might quote many instances: John Bunyan's *Pilgrim* may suffice instead of a hundred others; and this good text of ours, all mouldy and chill with the prison in which Jeremiah lay, hath nevertheless a brightness and a beauty about it, which it might never have had if it had not come as a cheering word to the prisoner of the Lord, shut up in the court of the prison-house.

God's people have always in their worst condition found out the best of their God. He is good at all times; but he seemeth to be at his best when they are at their worst. 'How could you bear your long imprisonment so well?' said one to the Landgrave of Hesse, who had been shut up for his attachment to the principles of the Reformation. He replied, 'The Divine consolations of martyrs were with me.' Doubtless there is a consolation more deep, more strong than any other, which God keeps for those who, being his faithful witnesses, have to endure exceeding great tribulation from the enmity of man. There is a glorious aurora for the frigid zone; and stars glisten in northern skies with unusual splendour. Rutherford had a quaint saying, that when he was cast into the cellars of affliction, he remembered that the great King always kept his wine there, and he began to seek at once for the wine bottles, and to drink of the 'wines on the lees well refined'.

They who dive in the sea of affliction bring up rare pearls. You know, my companions in affliction, that it is so. You whose bones have been ready to come through the skin through long lying upon the weary couch; you who have seen your earthly goods carried away from you, and have been reduced well nigh to penury; you who have gone to the grave yet seven times, till you have feared that your last earthly friend would be borne away by unpitying death; you have proved that he is a faithful God, and that as your tribulations abound, so your consolations also abound by Christ Jesus.

My prayer is, in taking this text this morning, that some other prisoners of the Lord may have its joyous promise spoken home to them; that you who are straitly shut up and cannot come forth by reason of present heaviness of spirit, may hear him say, as with a soft whisper in your ears, and in your hearts, 'Call unto me, and I will answer thee, and shew thee great and mighty things which thou knowest not.'

The text naturally splits itself up into three distinct particles of truth. Upon these let us speak as we are enabled by God the Holy Spirit. *Firstly*, prayer commanded - 'Call unto me'; *secondly*, an answer promised - 'And I will answer thee'; *thirdly*, faith encouraged - 'And shew thee great and mighty things which thou knowest not'.

1. Prayer Commanded

We are not merely counselled and recommended to pray, but bidden to pray. This is great condescension. A hospital is built: it is considered sufficient that free admission shall be given to the sick when they seek it; but no order in council is made that a man *must* enter its gates. A soup kitchen is well provided for in the depth of winter. Notice is promulgated that those who are poor may receive food on application; but no one thinks of passing an Act of Parliament compelling the poor to come and wait at the door to take the charity. It is thought to be enough to proffer it without issuing any sort of mandate that men *shall* accept it. Yet so strange is *the infatuation of man* on the one hand, which makes him need a command to be merciful to his own soul, and so marvellous is the condescension of our gracious God on the other, that he issues a command of love without which not a man of Adam born would partake of the gospel feast, but would rather starve than come. In the matter of prayer it is even so.

God's own people need, or else they would not receive it, a command to pray. How is this? Because, dear friends, we are very subject to *fits of worldliness*, if indeed that be not our usual state. We do not forget to eat: we do not forget to take the shop shutters down: we do not forget to be diligent in business: we do not forget to go to our beds to rest: but we often do forget to wrestle with God in prayer, and to spend, as we ought to spend, long periods in consecrated fellowship with our Father and our God. With too many professors the ledger is so bulky that you cannot move it, and the Bible, representing their devotion, is so small that you might almost put it in your waistcoat pocket. Hours for the world! Moments for Christ! The world has the best, and our closet the parings of our time. We give our strength and freshness to the ways of mammon, and our fatigue and languor to the ways of God. Hence it is that we need to be commanded to attend to that very act which ought to be our greatest happiness, as it is our highest privilege to perform, viz, to meet with our God. 'Call unto me,' saith he, for he knows that we are apt to forget to call upon God. 'What meanest thou, oh, sleeper? Arise and call upon thy God', is an exhortation which is needed by us as well as by Jonah in the storm.

He understands what *heavy hearts* we have sometimes, when under a sense of sin. Satan says to us, 'Why should you pray? How can you hope to prevail? In vain thou sayest, I will arise and go to my Father, for thou art not worthy to be one of his hired servants. How canst thou see the King's face after thou hast played the traitor against him? How wilt thou dare to approach unto the altar when thou hast thyself defiled it, and when the sacrifice which thou wouldst bring there is a poor polluted one?'

O brethren, it is well for us that we are commanded to pray, or else in times of heaviness we might give it up. If God command me, unfit as I may be, I will creep to the footstool of grace; and since he says, 'Pray without ceasing', though my words fail me and my heart itself will wander, yet I will stammer out the wishes of my hungering soul and say, 'O God, at least teach me to pray and help me to prevail with thee'.

Are we not commanded to pray also because of our *frequent unbelief*? Unbelief whispers, 'What profit is there if thou shouldst seek the Lord upon such and such a matter?' This is a case quite out of the list of those things wherein God hath interposed, and, therefore (saith the devil), if you were in any other position you might rest upon the mighty arm of God; but here your prayer will not avail you. Either it is too trivial a matter, or it is too connected with temporals, or else it is a matter in which you have sinned too much, or else it is too high, too hard, too complicated a piece of business, you have no right to take that before God! So suggests the foul fiend of hell.

Therefore, there stands written as an everyday precept suitable to every case into which a Christian can be cast, 'Call unto me - call unto me'.

Art thou sick? Wouldst thou be healed? Cry unto me, for I am a great Physician.

Does providence trouble thee? Art thou fearful that thou shalt not provide things honest in the sight of man? Call unto me!

Do thy children vex thee? Dost thou feel that which is sharper than an adder's tooth - a thankless child? Call unto me.

Are thy griefs little yet painful, like small points and pricks of thorns? Call unto me!

Is thy burden heavy as though it would make thy back break beneath its load? Call unto me!

'Cast thy burden upon the Lord, and he shall sustain thee; He shall never suffer the righteous to be moved.' In the valley - on the mountain - on the barren rock - in the briny sea, submerged, anon, beneath the billows, and lifted up by and by upon the crest of the waves - in the furnace when the coals are glowing - in the gates of death when the jaws of hell would shut themselves upon thee - cease thou not, for the commandment evermore addresses thee with 'Call unto me'. Still prayer is mighty and must prevail with God to bring thee thy deliverance. These are some of the reasons why the privilege of supplication is also in Holy Scripture spoken of as duty: there are many more, but these will suffice this morning.

We must not leave our first part till we have made another remark. We ought to be very glad that God hath given us this command *in his Word* that it may be sure and abiding. You may turn to fifty passages where the same precept is uttered. I do not often read in scripture, 'Thou shalt not kill'; 'Thou shalt not covet'. Twice the law is given, but I often read gospel precepts, for if the law be given twice, the gospel is given seventy times seven. For every precept which I cannot keep, by reason of my being weak through the flesh, I find a thousand precepts, which it is sweet and pleasant for me to keep, by reason of the power of the Holy Spirit which dwelleth in the children of God; and this command to pray is insisted upon again and again.

It may be a seasonable exercise for some of you to find out how often in scripture you are told to pray. You will be surprised to find how many times such words as these are given:

'Call upon me in the day of trouble, and I will deliver thee.'

'Ye people, pour out your heart before him'.

'Seek ye the Lord while he may be found; call ye upon him while he is near.'

'Ask, and it shall be given you; seek, and ye shall find; knock, and it shall be opened unto you.'

'Watch and pray lest ye enter into temptation.'

'Pray without ceasing.'

'Come boldly unto the throne of grace.'

'Draw nigh to God and he will draw nigh to you.'

'Continue in prayer.'

I need not multiply where I could not possibly exhaust. I pick two or three out of this great bag of pearls. Come, Christian, you ought never to question whether you have a right to pray: you should never ask, 'May I be permitted to come into his presence?' When you have so many commands (and God's commands are all promises, and all enablings), you may come boldly unto the throne of heavenly grace, by the new and living way through the rent veil.

But there are times when God not only commands his people to pray in the Bible, but he also commands them to pray directly *by the monitions of his Holy Spirit*. You who know the inner life comprehend me at once. You feel on a sudden, possibly in the midst of business, the pressing thought that you *must* retire to pray. It may be, you do not at first take particular notice of the inclination, but it comes again, and again, and again - 'Retire, and pray!' I find that in the matter of prayer, I am myself very much like a water-wheel which runs well when there is plenty of water, but which turns with very little force when the brook is running shallow; or, like the ship which flies over the waves, putting out all her canvas when the wind is favourable, but which has to tack about most laboriously when there is but little of the favouring breeze. Now, it strikes me that whenever our Lord gives you the special inclination to pray, that you should double your diligence.

You ought always to pray and not to faint; yet when he gives you the special longing after prayer, and you feel a peculiar aptness and enjoyment in it, you have, over and above the command which is constantly binding, another command which should compel you to cheerful obedience. At such times I think we may stand in the position of David, to whom the Lord said, 'When thou hearest a sound of a going in the tops of the mulberry trees, then shalt thou bestir thyself'. That going in the tops of the mulberry trees may have been the footfalls of angels hastening to the help of David, and then David was to smite the Philistines, and when God's mercies are coming, their footfalls are our desires to pray; and our desires to pray should be at once an indication that the set time to favour Zion is come. Sow plentifully now, for thy harvest is sure. Wrestle now, Jacob, for thou art about to be made a prevailing prince, and thy name shall be called Israel. Now is thy time, spiritual merchantmen; the market is high, trade much; thy profit shall be large. See to it that thou usest right well the golden hour, and reap thy harvest while the sun shines.

When we enjoy visitations from on high, we should be peculiarly constant in prayer; and if some other duty less pressing should have the go-by for a season, it will not be amiss and we shall be no loser; for when God bids us specially pray by the monitions of his Spirit, then should we bestir ourselves in prayer.

2. An Answer Promised

We ought not to tolerate for a minute the ghastly and grievous thought that God will not answer prayer. *His nature*, as manifested in Christ Jesus, demands it. He has revealed himself in the gospel as a God of love, full of grace and truth; and how can he refuse to help those of his creatures who humbly in his own appointed way seek his face and favour?

When the Athenian senate, upon one occasion, found it most convenient to meet together in the open air, as they were sitting in their deliberations, a sparrow, pursued by a hawk, flew in the direction of the senate. Being hard pressed by the bird of prey, it sought shelter in the bosom of one of the senators. He, being a man of rough and vulgar mould, took the bird from his bosom, dashed it on the ground and so killed it. Whereupon the whole senate rose in uproar, and without one single dissenting voice, condemned him to die, as being unworthy of a seat in the senate with them, or to be called an Athenian, if he did not render succour to a creature that confided in him.

Can we suppose that the God of heaven, whose nature is love, could tear out of his bosom the poor fluttering dove that flies from the eagle of justice into the bosom of his mercy? Will he give the invitation to us to seek his face, and when we, as he knows, with so much trepidation of fear, yet summon courage enough to fly into his bosom, will he then be unjust and ungracious enough to forget to hear our cry and to answer us? Let us not think so hardly of the God of heaven.

Let us recollect next, *his past character* as well as his nature. I mean the character which he has won for himself by his past deeds of grace.

Consider, my brethren, that one stupendous display of bounty - if I were to mention a thousand I could not give a better illustration of the character of God than that one deed: 'He that spared not his own Son, but freely delivered him up for us all' - and it is not my inference only, but the inspired conclusion of an apostle - 'how shall he not with him also freely give us all things?' If the Lord did not refuse to listen to my voice when I was a guilty sinner and an enemy, how can he disregard my cry now that I am justified and saved! How is it that he heard the voice of my misery when my heart knew it not, and would not seek relief, if after all he will not hear me now that I am his child, his friend? The streaming wounds of Jesus are the sure guarantees for answered prayer. George Herbert represents in that quaint poem of his, *The Bag*, the Saviour saying:

> If ye have anything to send or write
> (I have no bag, but here is room)
> Unto my Father's hands and sight,
> (Believe me) it shall safely come.
> That I shall mind what you impart
> Look, you may put it very near my heart,
> Or if hereafter any of friends
> Will use me in this kind, the door
> Shall still be open; what he sends
> I will present and somewhat more
> Not to his hurt.

Surely, George Herbert's thought was that the atonement was in itself a guarantee that prayer must be heard, that the great gash made near the Saviour's heart, which let the light into the very depths of the heart of Deity, was a proof that he who sits in heaven would hear the cry of his people. You misread Calvary, if you think that prayer is useless. But, beloved, we have *the Lord's own promise* for it, and he is a God that cannot lie. 'Call upon me in the day of trouble and I will answer thee'. Has he not said, 'Whatsoever ye shall ask in prayer, believe that ye shall have it and ye shall have it.' We cannot pray, indeed, unless we believe this doctrine; 'for he that cometh to God must believe that he is, and that he is the rewarder of them that diligently seek him'; and if we have any question at all about whether our prayer will be heard, we are comparable to him that wavereth; 'for he who wavereth is like a wave of the sea, driven with the wind and tossed; let not that man think that he shall receive anything of the Lord.'

Furthermore, it is not necessary, still it may strengthen the point, if we add that *our own experience* leads us to believe that God will answer prayer. I must not speak for you, but I may speak for myself. If there be anything I know, anything that I am quite assured of beyond all question, it is that praying breath is never spent in vain. If no other man here can say it, I dare to say it, and I know that I can prove it. My own conversion is the result of prayer, long, affectionate, earnest, importunate. Parents prayed for me; God heard their cries, and here I am to preach the gospel.

Since then I have adventured upon some things that were far beyond my capacity as I thought; but I have never failed, because I have cast myself upon the Lord. You know as a church that I have not scrupled to indulge large ideas of what we might do for God, and we have accomplished all that we purposed. I have sought God's aid, and assistance, and help, in all my manifold undertakings, and though I cannot tell here the story of my private life in God's work, yet if it were written it would be a standing proof that there is a God that answers prayer.

He has heard *my* prayers, not now and then, nor once nor twice, but so many times, that it has grown into a habit with me to spread my case before God with the absolute certainty that whatsoever I ask of God, he will give to me. It is not now a 'perhaps' or a possibility. I know that my Lord answers me, and I dare not doubt it, it were indeed folly if I did. As I am sure that a certain amount of leverage will lift a weight, so I know that a certain amount of prayer will get anything from God. As the rain-cloud brings the shower, so prayer brings the blessing. As spring scatters flowers, so supplication ensures mercies. In all labour there is profit, but most of all in the work of intercession: I am sure of this, for I have reaped it. As I put trust in the queen's money, and have never failed yet to buy what I want when I produce the cash, so put I trust in God's promises, and mean to do so till I find that he shall once tell me that they are base coin, and will not do to trade with in heaven's market.

But why should I speak? O brothers and sisters, you all know in your own selves that God hears prayer; if you do not, then where is your Christianity? Where is your religion? You will need to learn what are the first elements of the truth, for all saints, young or old, set it down as certain that he doth hear prayer.

Still remember that prayer is always to be offered in submission to God's will; that when we say, God heareth prayer, we do not intend by that, that he always gives us literally what we ask for. We do mean, however, this, that he gives us what is best for us; and that if he does not give us the mercy we ask for in silver, he bestows it upon us in gold. If he doth not take away the thorn in the flesh, yet he saith, 'My grace is sufficient for thee', and that comes to the same in the end.

Lord Bolingbroke said to the Countess of Huntingdon, 'I cannot understand, your Ladyship, how you can make out earnest prayer to be consistent with submission to the Divine will'. 'My Lord,' she said, 'that is a matter of no difficulty. If I were a courtier of some generous king, and he gave me permission to ask any favour I pleased of him, I should be sure to put it thus, "Will your majesty be graciously pleased to grant me such-and-such a favour; but at the same time though I very much desire it, if it would in any way detract from your majesty's honour, or if in your majesty's judgment it should seem better that I did not have this favour, I shall be quite as content to go without it as to receive it." So you see I might earnestly offer a petition, and yet I might submissively leave it in the king's hands.'

So with God. We never offer up prayer without inserting that clause, either in spirit or in words, 'Nevertheless, not as I will, but as thou wilt; not my will, but thine be done.' We can only pray without an 'if' when we are quite sure that our will must be God's will, because God's will is fully our will. A much-slandered poet has well said:

'Man, regard thy prayers as a purpose of love to thy soul,
Esteem the providence that led to them as an index of God's
  good will;
So shalt thou pray aright, and thy words shall meet with
  acceptance.
Also, in pleading for others, be thankful for the fullness of thy
  prayer;

For if thou art ready to ask, the Lord is more ready to bestow.
The salt preserveth the sea, and the saints uphold the earth;
Their prayers are the thousand pillars that prop the canopy of nature.
Verily, an hour without prayer, from some terrestrial mind,
Were a curse in the calendar of time, a spot of the blackness of darkness.
Perchance the terrible day, when the world must rock into ruins,
Will be one unwhitened by prayer - shall he find faith on the earth?
For there is an economy of mercy, as of wisdom, and power, and means;
Neither is one blessing granted, unbesought from the treasury of good:
And the charitable heart of the Being, to depend upon whom is happiness.
Never withholdeth a bounty, so long as his subject prayeth;
Yea, ask what thou wilt, to the second throne in heaven,
It is thine for whom it was appointed; there is no limit unto prayer:
But and if thou cease to ask, tremble, thou self-suspended creatures,
For thy strength is cut off as was Samson's: and the hour of thy doom is come.'

3. I come to our third point, which I think is full of encouragement to all those who exercise the hallowed art of prayer: **Encouragement to Faith**, 'I will shew thee great and mighty things which thou knowest not'.

Let us just remark that this was originally spoken to a prophet in prison; and therefore, it applies in the first place to *every teacher*; and, indeed, as every teacher must be a learner, it has a bearing upon *every learner* in divine truth. The best way by which a prophet and teacher and learner can know the reserved truths, the higher and more mysterious truths of God, is by waiting upon God in prayer. I noticed very specially yesterday in reading the Book of the Prophet Daniel, how Daniel found out Nebuchadnezzar's dream. The soothsayers, the magicians, the astrologers of the Chaldees brought out their curious books and their strange-looking instruments, and began to mutter their *abracadabra* and all sorts of mysterious incantations, but they all failed. What did Daniel do? He set himself to prayer, and knowing that the prayer of a united body of men has more prevalence than the prayer of one, we find that Daniel called together his brethren, and bade them unite with him in earnest prayer that God would be pleased of his infinite mercy to open up the vision. 'Then Daniel went to his house, and made the thing known to Hananiah, Mishael, and Azariah, his companions, that they would desire mercies of the God of heaven concerning this secret, that Daniel and his fellows should not perish with the rest of the wise men of Babylon.'

And in the case of John who was the Daniel of the New Testament, you remember he saw a book in the right hand of him that sat on the throne - a book sealed with seven seals which none was found worthy to open or to look thereon. What did John do? The book was by and by opened by the Lion of the Tribe of Judah, who had prevailed to open the book; but it is written first before the book was opened, 'I wept much'. Yes, and the tears of John which were his liquid prayers were, as far as he was concerned, the sacred keys by which the folded book was opened.

Brethren in the ministry, you who are teachers in the Sabbath-school, and all of you who are learners in the college of Jesus Christ, I pray you remember that prayer is your best means of study: like Daniel you shall understand the dream, and the interpretation thereof, when you have sought unto

God; and like John you shall see the seven seals of precious truth unloosed, after that you have wept much. 'Yea, if thou criest after knowledge, and liftest up the voice for understanding; if thou seekest her as silver, and searchest for her as for hid treasures; then shalt thou understand the fear of the Lord and find the knowledge of God'. Stones are not broken, except by an earnest use of the hammer, and the stone-breaker usually goes down on his knees. Use the hammer of diligence, and let the knee of prayer be exercised, too, and there is not a stony doctrine in Revelation which is useful for you to understand, which will not fly into shivers under the exercise of prayer and faith.

'*Bene orasse est bene studuisse*' was a wise sentence of Luther, which has been so often quoted that we hardly venture but to hint at it. 'To have prayed well is to have studied well.' You may force your way through anything with the leverage of prayers. Thoughts and reasonings may be like the steel wedges which may open a way into truth; but prayer is the lever, the prise which forces open the iron chest of sacred mystery, that we may get the treasure that is hidden therein for those who can force their way to reach it. The kingdom of heaven still suffereth violence, and the violent taketh it by force. Take care that ye work away with the mighty implement of prayer, and nothing can stand against you.

We must not, however, stop there. We have applied the text to only one case; it is applicable to a hundred. We single out another. *The saint may expect to discover deeper experience* and to know more of the higher life and scriptural life, by being much in prayer. There are different translations of my text. One version renders it, 'I will shew thee great and fortified things which thou knowest not.' Another reads it, 'Great and reserved things which thou knowest not.' Now, all the developments of spiritual life are not alike easy of attainment.

There are the common frames and feelings of repentance, and faith, and joy, and hope, which are enjoyed by the entire family: but there is an upper realm of rapture, of communion, and conscious union with Christ which is far from being the common dwelling-place of believers. All believers see Christ; but all believers do not put their fingers into the prints of the nails, nor thrust their hand into his side. We have not all the high privilege of John to lean upon Jesus' bosom, nor of Paul, to be caught up into the third heaven. In the ark of salvation, we find a lower, second and third storey; all are in the ark, but all are not in the same storey. Most Christians, as to the river of experience, are only up to the ankles; some others have waded till the stream is up to the knees; a few find it breast-high; and but a few - oh! how few! - find it a river to swim in, the bottom of which they cannot touch.

My brethren, there are heights in experimental knowledge of the things of God which the eagle's eye of acumen and philosophic thought hath never seen; and there are secret paths which the lion's whelp of reason and judgment hath not as yet learned to travel. God alone can bear us there; but the chariot in which he takes us up, and the fiery steeds with which that chariot is dragged are prevailing prayers.

Prevailing prayer is victorious over the God of mercy: 'By his strength he had power with God: yea, he had power over the angel, and prevailed: he wept, and made supplication unto him: he found him in Beth-el, and there he spake with us.'

Prevailing prayer takes the Christian to Carmel, and enables him to cover heaven with clouds of blessing, and earth with floods of mercy.

Prevailing prayer bears the Christian aloft to Pisgah and

shows him the inheritance reserved; ay, and it elevates him to Tabor and transfigures him, till in the likeness of his Lord, as he is, so are we also in this world.

If you would reach to something higher than ordinary grovelling experience, look to the Rock that is higher than you, and look with the eye of faith through the windows of importunate prayer. To grow in experience then, there must be much prayer.

You must have patience with me while I apply this text to two or three more cases. It is certainly true of *the sufferer under trial*: if he waits upon God in prayer much he shall receive greater deliverances than he has ever dreamed of - 'great and mighty things which thou knowest not'.

Here is Jeremiah's testimony: 'Thou drewest near in the day that I called upon thee: thou saidst, Fear not. O Lord, thou hast pleaded the causes of my soul; thou hast redeemed my life.'

And David's is the same: 'I called upon the Lord in distress: the Lord answered me, and set me in a large place... I will praise thee for thou hast heard me, and art become my salvation.' And yet again: 'Then they cried unto the Lord in their trouble, and he delivered them out of their distresses. And he led them forth by the right way, that they might go to a city of habitation.'

'My husband is dead,' said the poor woman, 'and my creditor is come to take my two sons as bondsmen.' She hoped that Elijah would possibly say, 'What are your debts? I will pay them.' Instead of that, he multiplies her oil till it is written, 'Go thou and pay thy debts, and' - what was the 'and'? - 'live thou and thy children upon the rest.'

So often it will happen that God will not only help his people through the miry places of the way, so that they may just stand on the other side of the slough, but he will bring them safely on the journey. That was a remarkable miracle, when in the midst of the storm, Jesus Christ came walking upon the sea, the disciples received him into the ship, and not only was the sea calm, but it is recorded, 'Immediately the ship was at the land whither they went.' That was a mercy over and above what they asked.

I sometimes hear you pray and make use of a quotation which is not in the Bible: 'He is able to do exceeding abundantly above what we *can* ask or even think.' It is not so written in the Bible. I do not know what we can ask or what we can think. But it is said, 'He is able to do exceeding abundantly above what we ask or even think.' Let us then, dear friends, when we are in a great trial only say, 'Now I am in prison; like Jeremiah I will pray, for I have God's command to do it; and I will look out as he did, expecting that he will show me reserved mercies which I know nothing of at present.' He will not merely bring his people through the battle, covering their heads in it, but he will bring them forth with banners waving, to divide the spoil with the mighty, and to claim their portion with the strong. Expect great things of a God who gives such great promises as these.

Again, *here is encouragement for the worker*. Most of you are doing something for Christ; I am happy to be able to say this, knowing that I do not flatter you. My dear friends, wait upon God much in prayer, and you have the promise that he will do greater things for you than you know of. We know not how much capacity for usefulness there may be in us. That ass's jawbone lying there upon the earth, what can it do? Nobody knows what it can do. It gets into Samson's hands, what can it not do? No one knows what it cannot do now that a Samson wields it.

And you, friend, have often thought yourself to be as contemptible as that bone, and you have said, 'What can I do?' Ay, but when Christ by his Spirit grips you, what can you not do? Truly you may adopt Paul's language and say, 'I can do all things through Christ who strengtheneth me.' However, do not depend upon prayer without effort.

In a certain school there was one girl who knew the Lord, a very gracious, simple-hearted, trustful child. As usual, grace developed itself in the child according to the child's position. Her lessons were always best said of any in the class. Another girl said to her, 'How is it that your lessons are so well said?' 'I pray God to help me,' she said, 'to learn my lesson.' Well, thought the other, then I will do the same. The next morning when she stood up in the class she knew nothing; and when she was in disgrace she complained to the other, 'Why I prayed God to help me learn my lesson and I do not know anything of it. What is the use of prayer?' 'But did you sit down and try to learn it?' 'Oh! no,' she said, 'I never looked at the book.' 'Ah,' then said the other, 'I asked God to help me to learn my lesson; but I then sat down to it studiously, and I kept at it till I knew it well, and I learned it easily, because my earnest desire, which I had expressed to God was, Help me to be diligent in endeavouring to do my duty.'

So is it with some who come up to prayer-meetings and pray, and then they fold their arms and go away hoping that God's work will go on. Like the Negro woman singing, 'Fly abroad, thou mighty gospel', but not putting a penny in the plate; so that her friend touched her and said, 'But how can it fly if you don't give it wings to fly with?' There be many who appear to be very mighty in prayer, wondrous in supplications; but then they require God to do what they can do themselves, and, therefore, God does nothing at all for them.

'I shall leave my camel untied,' said an Arab once to Mahomet, 'and trust to providence.' 'Tie it up tight,' said Mahomet, 'and then trust to providence.' So you that say, 'I shall pray and trust my church, or my class, or my work to God's goodness,' may rather hear the voice of experience and wisdom which says, 'Do thy best; work as if all rested upon thy toil; as if thy own arm would bring thy salvation'; 'and when thou hast done all, cast thyself on him without whom it is in vain to rise up early and to sit up late, and to eat the bread of carefulness; and if he speed thee give him the praise.'

I shall not detain you many minutes longer, but I want to notice that this promise ought to prove useful for the comforting of those who are intercessors for others. You who are calling upon God to save your children, to bless your neighbours, to remember your husbands or your wives in mercy, may take comfort from this, 'I will shew thee great and might things, which thou knowest not'.

A celebrated minister in the last century, one Mr Bailey, was the child of a godly mother. This mother had almost ceased to pray for her husband, who was a man of a most ungodly stamp, and a bitter persecutor. The mother prayed for her boy, and while he was yet eleven or twelve years of age, eternal mercy met with him. So sweetly instructed was the child in all things of the kingdom of God, that the mother requested him - and for some time he always did so - to conduct family prayer in the house. Morning and evening this little one laid open the Bible; and though the father would not deign to stop for the family prayer, yet on one occasion he was rather curious to know 'what sort of an out the boy would make of it', so he stopped on the other side of the door, and God blessed the prayer of his own child under thirteen years of age to his conversion. The mother might well have read my text with streaming eyes, and said, 'Yes, Lord, thou hast shewn me great and mighty things which I knew not; thou hast not only saved my boy, but through my boy thou hast brought my husband to the truth.'

You cannot guess how greatly God will bless you. Only go and stand at his door, you cannot tell what is in reserve for you. If you do not beg at all, you will get nothing; but if you beg he may not only give you, as it were, the bones and broken meat, but he may say to the servant at his table, 'Take thou that dainty meat, and set that before the poor man'.

Ruth went to glean; she expected to get a few good ears: but Boaz said, 'Let her glean even among the sheaves, and rebuke her not'; he said moreover to her, 'At meal-times come thou hither, and eat of the bread, and dip thy morsel in the vinegar.' Nay, she found a husband where she only expected to find a handful of barley. So in prayer for others, God may give us such mercies that we shall be astounded at them, since we expected but little.

Hear what is said of Job, and learn its lesson, 'And the Lord said, My servant Job shall pray for you: for him will I accept: lest I deal with you after your folly, in that ye have not spoken of me the thing which is right, like my servant Job. ...And the Lord turned the captivity of Job, when he prayed for his friends: also the Lord gave Job twice as much as he had before.'

Now, this word to close with. Some of you are seekers for your own conversion. God has quickened you to solemn prayer about your own souls. You are not content to go to hell, you want heaven; you want washing in the precious blood; you want eternal life. Dear friends, I pray you take this text - God himself speaks it to you - 'Call unto me, and I will answer thee, and shew thee great and mighty things, which thou knowest not.' At once take God at his word. Get home, go into your chamber and shut the door, and try him.

Young man, I say, try the Lord. Young woman, prove him, see whether he be true or not. If God be true, you cannot seek mercy at his hands through Jesus Christ and get a negative reply. He must, for his own promise and character bind him to it, open mercy's gate to you who knock with all your heart. God help you, believing in Christ Jesus, to cry aloud unto God, and his answer of peace is already on the way to meet you. You shall hear him say, 'Your sins which are many are all forgiven.'

The Lord bless you for his love's sake. Amen.

PRAYERS

PRAYER 1

Help from on High

O thou who art King of kings and Lord of lords, we worship thee.

> Before Jehovah's awful throne
> We bow with sacred joy.

We can truly say that we delight in God. There was a time when we feared thee, O God, with the fear of bondage. Now we reverence, but we love as much as we reverence. The thought of thine omnipresence was once horrible to us. We said: 'Whither shall we flee from his presence?' and it seemed to make hell itself more dreadful, because we heard a voice, 'If I make my bed in hell, behold thou art there.' But now, O Lord, we desire to find thee. Our longing is to feel thy presence, and it is the heaven of heavens that thou art there. The sick bed is soft when thou art there. The furnace of affliction grows cool when thou art there, and the house of prayer when thou art present is none other than the house of God, and it is the very gate of heaven.

Come near, our Father, come very near to thy children. Some of us are very weak in body and faint in heart. Soon, O God, lay thy right hand upon us and say unto us, 'Fear not'. Peradventure, some of us are alike, and the world is attracting us. Come near to kill the influence of the world with thy superior power.

Even to worship may not seem easy to some. The dragon seems to pursue them, and floods out of his mouth wash away their devotion. Give to them great wings as of an eagle, that each one may fly away into the place prepared for him, and rest in the presence of God today.

Our Father, come and rest thy children now. Take the helmet from our brow, remove from us the weight of our heavy armour for a while, and may we just have peace, perfect peace, and be at rest. Oh! help us, we pray thee, now. As thou hast already washed thy people in the fountain filled with blood and they are clean, now this morning wash us from defilement in the water. With the basin and with the ewer, O Master, wash our feet again. It will greatly refresh; it will prepare us for innermost fellowship with thyself. So did the priests wash ere they went into the holy place.

Lord Jesus, take from us now everything that would hinder the closest communion with God. Any wish or desire that might hamper us in prayer remove, we pray thee. Any memory of either sorrow or care that might hinder the fixing of our affection wholly on our God, take it away now. What have we to do with idols any more? Thou hast seen and observed us. Thou knowest where the difficulty lies. Help us against it, and may we now come boldly, not into the holy place alone, but into the holiest of all, where we should not dare to come if our great Lord had not rent the veil, sprinkled the mercy seat with his own blood, and bidden us enter.

Now, we have come close up to thyself, to the light that shineth between the wings of the cherubim, and we speak with thee now as a man speaketh with his friends. Our God, we are thine. Thou art ours. We are now concerned in one business, we are leagued together for one battle. Thy battle is our battle, and our fight is thine. Help us, we pray thee. Thou who didst strengthen Michael and his angels to cast out the dragon and his angels, help poor flesh and blood that to us also the word may be fulfilled: 'The Lord shall bruise Satan under your feet, shortly.'

Our Father, we are very weak. Worst of all we are very wicked if left to ourselves, and we soon fall a prey to the enemy. Therefore help us. We confess that sometimes in prayer when we are nearest to thee at that very time some evil thought comes in, some wicked desire. Oh! what poor simpletons we are. Lord, help us. We feel as if we would now come closer to thee still, and hide under the shadow of thy wings. We wish to be lost in God. We pray that thou mayest live in us, and not we live, but Christ live in us and show himself in us and through us.

Lord, sanctify us. Oh! that thy Spirit might come and saturate every faculty, subdue every passion, and use every power of our nature for obedience to God.

Come, Holy Spirit, we do know thee; thou hast often overshadowed us. Come, more fully take possession of us. Standing now as we feel we are right up at the mercy seat our very highest prayer is for perfect holiness, complete consecration, entire cleansing from evil. Take our heart, our head, our hands, our feet, and use us all for thee. Lord, take our substance, let us not hoard it for ourselves, nor spend it for ourselves. Take our talent, let us not try to educate ourselves that we may have the repute of being wise, but let every gain of mental attainment be still that we may serve thee better.

May every breath be for thee; may every minute be spent for thee. Help us to live while we live and while we are busy in the world as we must be, for we are called to it, may we sanctify the world for thy service. May we be lumps of salt in the midst of society. May our spirit and temper as well as our conversation be heavenly; may there be an influence about us that shall make the world the better before we leave it. Lord, hear us in this thing.

And now that we have thine ear we would pray for this poor world in which we live. We are often horrified by it. O Lord, we could wish that we did not know anything about it for our own comfort. We have said, 'Oh! for a lodge in some vast wilderness'. We hear of oppression and robbery and murder, and men seem let loose against each other. Lord, have mercy upon this great and wicked city. What is to be done with these millions? What can we do? At least help every child of thine to do his utmost. May none of us contribute to the evil directly or indirectly, but may we contribute to the good that is in it.

We feel we may speak with thee now about this, for when thy servant Abraham stood before thee and spake with such wonderful familiarity to thee, he pleaded for Sodom; and we plead for London. We would follow the example of the father of the faithful and pray for all great cities, and indeed for all the nations. Lord, let thy kingdom come. Send forth thy light and thy truth. Chase the old dragon from his throne, with all his hellish crew. Oh! that the day might come when even upon earth the Son of the woman, the Man-child, should rule the nations, not with a broken staff of wood, but with an enduring sceptre of iron, full of mercy, full of power, full of grace, but yet irresistible. Oh! that that might soon come, the personal advent of our Lord! We long for the millennial triumph of his Word.

Until then, O Lord, gird us for the fight, and make us to be among those who overcome through the blood of the Lamb and through the word of our testimony, because we 'love not our lives unto the death'.

We lift our voice to thee in prayer also for all our dear ones. Lord, bless the sick and make them well as soon as it is right they should be. Sanctify to them all they have to bear. There are also dear friends who are very weak; some that are very trembling. God bless them. While the tent is being taken down may the inhabitant within look on with calm joy, for we shall by and by 'be clothed upon with our house that is from heaven'. Lord, help us to sit very loose by all these things here below. May we live here like strangers and make the world not a house but an inn, in which we sup and lodge, expecting to be on our journey tomorrow.

Lord save the unconverted, and bring out, we pray thee, from among them those who are converted, but who have not confessed Christ. May the church be built up by many who, having believed, are baptised unto the sacred name. We pray thee go on and multiply the faithful in the land. Oh! that thou wouldst turn the hearts of men to the gospel once more. Thy servant is often very heavy in heart because of the departures from the faith. Oh! bring them back; let not Satan take away any more of the stars with his tail, but may the lamps of God shine bright. Oh! thou that walkest among the seven golden candlesticks trim the flame, pour forth the oil, and let the light shine brightly and steadily. Now, Lord, we cannot pray any longer, though we have a thousand things to ask for. Thy servant cannot, so he begs to leave a broken prayer at the mercy seat with this at the foot of it: We ask in the name of Jesus Christ thy Son. Amen.

PRAYER 2

Thanks be unto God

O Lord God, help us now really to worship thee. We would thank thee for this occasion. We bless thy name for setting apart this hallowed season. Lord, wilt thou shut the door upon the world for us? Help us to forget our cares. Enable us to rise clean out of this world. May we get rid of all its down-dragging tendencies. May the attractions of these grosser things be gone, and do thou catch us away to thyself.

We do not ask to be entranced nor to see an angel in shining apparel, but we do ask that by faith we may see Jesus, and may his presence be so evidently realised among us that we may rejoice as well as if our eyes beheld him, and love him and trust him and worship him as earnestly as we should do if we could now put our fingers into the print of the nails.

O, thou precious Lord Jesus Christ, we do adore thee with all our hearts. Thou art Lord of all. We bless thee for becoming man that thou mightest be our next of kin, and being next of kin we bless thee for taking us into marriage union with thyself and for redeeming us and our inheritance from the captivity into which we were sold. Thou hast paid thy life for thy people; thou hast ransomed thy folk with thy heart's blood. Be thou, therefore, forever beloved and adored.

And now thou art not here for thou art risen. Our souls would track the shining way by which thou hast ascended through the gate of pearl up to thy Father's throne. We seem to see thee sitting there, man yet God, reigning over all things for thy people, and our ears almost catch the accents of the everlasting song which rolls up at thy feet: 'Worthy is the Lamb that was slain to receive honour, and power, and glory, and dominion, and might forever and ever.' Lord, we say, 'Amen'. From the outskirts of the crowd that surround thy throne we lift up our feeble voices in earnest 'Amens', for thou wast slain and hast redeemed us to God by thy blood and hast made us kings and priests unto God, and we shall reign with thee, for though far off by space, we know that we are very near to thy heart.

Thou lookest over the heads of the angelic squadrons to behold us, and thou dost hear the praises - aye, and the groans of thy well-beloved, for are not we most near thee, thy flesh and thy bones? We know we are. We feel the ties of kinship within us. We our best Beloved's are, and he is ours, and we are longing to get through the crowd that surround him, and to get to the forefront, and there to bow prostrate at the dear feet that were nailed to the tree for us, and worship the Lamb who liveth for ever and ever, who has prevailed to take the book and loose the seven seals thereof, to whom be glory, world without end. Hallelujah!

O Saviour, accept these our poor praises. They come from those thou lovest, and as we prize any little things that come from those we love, so do we feel that thou wilt accept the thanksgiving, the reverential homage of thy people, redeemed ones who are a people near unto thee, whose names are graven on the palms of thy hands, of whom thou art the active head and for whom thy heart beats true and full of love e'en now.

Oh, we can say we love thee; we wish we loved thee more; but thou art very dear to us. There is nought on earth like thee.

For the love of thy name we would live and die. If we think we love thee more than we do, we pray that we may love thee more than we think. Oh, take these hearts right away and unite them with thine own, and be thou heart and soul and life and everything to us; for whom have we in heaven but thee, and there is none upon earth we desire beside thee.

We worship the Father, we worship the Son, we worship the Holy Ghost with all the powers of our being. We fall prostrate before the awful yet glorious throne of the Infinite Majesty of heaven. The Lord accept us since we offer these praises in the name of Jesus.

And now most blessed Lord, look down upon those who do not love thee. O Redeemer, look upon them with those eyes of thine which are as flames of fire. Let them see how ill they treat thee. May they consider within themselves how dire is the ingratitude which can be negligent of a Saviour's blood, indifferent from a Saviour's heart. Oh, bring the careless and the godless to seek for mercy. Let those that are postponing serious things begin to see that the very thought of postponement of the claims of Christ is treason against his majesty. O Saviour, dart thy arrows abroad and let them wound many that they may fall down before thee and cry out for mercy.

But there are some who are wounded, broken hearts that seek peace - men and women, like Cornelius, that want to hear the words which God commands.

Oh, come divine Physician, and bind up every broken bone. Come with thy sacred nard which thou hast compounded of thine own heart's blood, and lay it home to the wounded conscience, and let it feel its power. Oh! give peace to those whose conscience is like the troubled sea which cannot rest.

O God, our God, let not the teaching of the Sunday-school,

the preaching of the evangelists, the personal visitations of individual minds, let not any of these efforts be in vain. Do give conversions. We groan out this prayer from our very heart, yet can we also sing it, for thou hast heard us plenteously already, and our heart doth rejoice in God the Saviour who worketh so graciously among the children of men.

We have been astonished as the Holy Ghost has fallen even upon the chief of sinners, and men afar off from God have been brought in. But, Lord, do more of this among us. Let us see greater things than these. Where we have had one saved, let us have an hundred to the praise of the glorious name of the Well-beloved.

Lord, keep us all from sin; teach us how to talk circumspectly; enable us to guard our minds against error of doctrine, our hearts against wrong feelings, and our lives against evil actions. Oh, may we never speak unadvisedly with our lips, nor give way to anger. Above all, keep us from covetousness which is idolatry, and from malice which is of the devil. Grant unto us to be full of sweetness and light. May love dwell in us and reign in us. May we look not every man on his own things, but every man on the things of others. Give us to live for Jesus. There is no life like it. Help us to be Christly men, Christ's men, and may we in all things reflect the light which we receive from him.

Bless our beloved church and all its organisations. O God, take care of it. Oh! do thou make every member of the church a pastor over others. Let all strive together for the good of all, and so may thy kingdom come among us.

And do thou prosper all the churches of Jesus Christ. What we ask for ourselves we seek for them. Let missionaries especially be helped by thy Spirit, and may there come a day in which the minds of men may be better prepared to receive the gospel, and may Messiah's kingdom come to the overthrow of her that sitteth on the Seven Hills and to the eternal waning of Mohammed's moon, to the overthrow of every idol, that Christ alone may reign. Our whole heart comes out in this. Reign, Immanuel, reign; sit on the high throne; ride on thy white horse; and let the armies of heaven follow thee, conquering and to conquer. Come, Lord Jesus; even so, come quickly. Amen and amen.

PRAYER 3

The Love without Measure or End

Lord, we would come to thee, but do thou come to us. Draw us and we will run after thee. Blessed Spirit, help our infirmities, for we know not what we should pray for as we ought. Come, Holy Spirit, and give right thoughts and right utterance that we may all be able to pray in the common prayer, the whole company feeling that for each one there is a portion. We are grateful as we remember that if the minister in the sanctuary should not be able to pray for any one of us there is one who bears the names of all his redeemed upon his breast, and upon his shoulder, who will take care with the love of his heart and the power of his arm to maintain the cause of all his own.

Dear Saviour, we put ourselves under thy sacred patronage. Advocate with the Father, plead for us this day, yea, make intercession for the transgressors. We desire to praise the name of the Lord with our whole heart, so many of us as have tasted that the Lord is gracious. Truly thou hast delivered us from the gulf of dark despair, wherein we wretched sinners lay. Thou hast brought us up also out of the horrible pit and out of the miry clay, thou hast set our feet upon a rock and the new song which thou hast put into our mouths we would not stifle, but we would bless the Lord whose mercy endureth forever.

We thank thee, Lord, for the love without beginning which chose us or ever the earth was, for the love without measure which entered into covenant for our redemption, for the love without failure which in due time appeared in the person of Christ and wrought out our redemption, for that love which has never changed, though we have wandered; that love which abideth faithful even when we are unfaithful.

O God, we praise thee for keeping us till this day, and for the full assurance that thou wilt never let us go. Some can say, 'He restoreth my soul', they had wandered, wandered sadly, but thou hast brought them back again. Lord, keep us from wandering, then will we sing, 'Unto him that is able to keep us from stumbling and to present us faultless before his presence with exceeding joy'. Bless the Lord, our inmost soul blesses the Lord. Blessed be the Father, the Son, and the Holy Spirit, the Triune; blessed be the Lord for every office sustained by each divine person, and for the divine blessing which has come streaming down to us through each one of those condescending titles worn by the Father, Son and the Holy Spirit.

We feel like singing all the time; we would take down our harp from the willows, if we had hung it there, and we would waken every string to the sweetest melody of praise unto the Lord our God. Yet, Lord, we cannot close with praise, for we are obliged to come before thee with humble confession of sin. We are not worthy of the least of all these favours; we cannot say, 'He is worthy for whom thou shouldst do this thing', nay, but we are altogether unworthy, and thy gifts are according to the riches of thy grace, for which again we praise thee.

Lord, forgive us all our sin. May thy pardoned ones have a renewed sense of their acceptance in the Beloved. If any cloud has arisen to hide thee from any believing eye, take that cloud away. If in our march through this world, so full of mire as it is, we have any spot on us, dear Saviour, wash our feet with that blessed foot-bath, and then say to us, 'Ye are clean every whit'. May we know it so, that there is no condemnation, no separation; sin is removed as to its separating as well as its destroying power, and may we enter into full fellowship with God. May we walk in the light as God is in the light, and have fellowship with him, while the blood of Jesus Christ, his Son, cleanseth us from all sin. Let no child of thine have any dead work upon his conscience, and may our conscience be purged from dead works to serve the living and true God.

And oh! if there are any that after having made the profession of religion have gone astray by any form of sin, Lord, restore them. If they have fallen by strong drink, if they have fallen by unchastity, if they have fallen by dishonesty, if, in any way, they have stained their garments, oh! that thy mighty grace might bring them back and put them yet among thy children. But give them not up, set them not as Admah, make them not as Zeboim, but let thy repentings be kindled and thy bowels of compassion be moved for them, and let them also be moved, and may they return with weeping and with supplication, and find thee a God ready to pardon.

Furthermore we ask of thee, our Father, this day to perfect thy work within our hearts. We are saved, but we would be saved from sin of every form and degree; from sins that lie within, and we are scarcely aware that they are there. If we have any pride of which we are not conscious, any unbelief of which we are not aware, if there is a clinging to the creature, a form of idolatry which we have not yet perceived, we pray thee, Lord, to search us as with candles till thou dost spy out the evil and then put it away. We are not satisfied with pardoned sin, we pray, 'Create in me a clean heart, O God, and renew a right spirit within me'. Help us in our daily life, in our families, in our relations as husbands or wives, parents or children, masters or servants, in our business transactions with our fellow men, in our dealings with the church of God, may we be true, upright, pure; kept from the great transgression because we are kept from the minor ones.

Oh! that we may be such as glorify Christ. Save us, we pray thee, from the common religion; give us the peculiar grace of a peculiar people. May we abide in Christ, may we live near to God. Let not the frivolities of the world have any power over us whatever. May we be too full grown in grace to be bewitched with the toys which are only becoming in children. Oh! give us to serve thee, and especially, and this prayer we have already prayed but we pray it again, make us useful in the salvation of our fellow man. O Lord, have we lived so long in the world and yet are our children unconverted? May we never rest until they are truly saved. Have we been going up and down in business, and are those round about us as yet unaware of our Christian character? Have we never spoken to them the Word of Life? Lord, arouse us to a deep concern for all with whom we come in contact from day to day. Make us all missionaries at home or in the street, or in our workshop, wherever providence has cast our lot, may we there shine as lights in the world.

Lord, keep us right, true in doctrine, true in experience, true in life, true in word, true in deed. Let us have an intense agony of spirit concerning the many who are going down to the everlasting fire of which our Master spoke. *Lord, save them*! LORD, SAVE THEM! Stay, we pray thee, the torrents of sin that run down the streets of London; purge the dead sea of sin, in which so many of the heathen are lying asoak. Oh!

that the day were come when the name of Jesus shall be a household word, when everybody knew of his love, and of his death, and of his blood, and of its cleansing power. Lord, save men, gather out the company of the redeemed people; let those whom the Father gave to Christ be brought out from among the ruins of the fall to be his joy and crown. 'Let the people praise thee, O God, yea, let all the people praise thee.' Let the ends of the earth fear him who died to save them. Let the whole earth be filled with the glory of God.

This is our great prayer, and we crown it with this: Come, Lord Jesus, come Lord and tarry not! Come in the fullness of thy power and the splendour of thy glory! Come quickly, even so come quickly, Lord Jesus. Amen.

PRAYER 4

The All-prevailing Plea

O Lord God! the fountain of all fullness, we, who are nothing but emptiness, come unto thee for all supplies, nor shall we come in vain, since we bear with us a plea which is all prevalent. Since we come commanded by thy Word, encouraged by thy promise, and preceded by Christ Jesus, our great high priest, we know that whatsoever we shall ask in prayer, believing, we shall receive. Only do thou help us now to ask right things, and may the utterances of our mouth be acceptable in thy sight, O God our strength and our redeemer.

We would first adore thy blessed and ever-to-be-beloved Name. 'All the earth doth worship thee, the Father everlasting.' Heaven is full of thy glory. Oh! that men's hearts were filled therewith, that the noblest creatures thou hast made, whom thou didst set in the paradise of God, for whom the Saviour shed his blood, loved thee with all their hearts.

The faithful, chosen, called and separated join in the everlasting song. All thy redeemed praise thee, O God! As the God of our election we extol thee for thine everlasting and immutable love. As the God and Father of our Lord Jesus Christ we bless thee for that unspeakable gift, the offering of thine Only-begotten. Words are but air, and tongues but clay, and thy compassion is divine, therefore it is not possible that any words of ours should 'reach the height of this great argument', or sound forth thy worthy praise for this superlative deed of grace.

We bless thee, also, divine Son of God, co-equal and co-eternal with the Father, that thou didst not disdain to be born of the Virgin, and that, being found in fashion like a man, thou didst not refuse to be obedient unto death, even the death of the cross. Let thy brows be girt with something better than thorns; let the eternal diadem forever glitter there. Thou wast slain, and hast redeemed us to God by thy blood; unto thee be glory, and honour, and power, and majesty, and dominion, and might, for ever and ever!

And equally, most blessed Spirit, thou who didst brood over chaos and bring it into order, thou who didst beget the Son of God's body of flesh, thou who didst quicken us to spiritual life, by whose divine energy we are sanctified, and hope to be made meet to be partakers of the inheritance of the saints in light, unto thee, also, be hallelujahs, world without end!

O Lord! our soul longeth for words of fire, but we cannot reach them! Oh! when shall we drop this clay which now is so uncongenial to our song? When shall we be able with wings to mount upwards to thy throne, and having learned some flaming sonnets that have once been sung by cherubim above, we shall praise thee for ever?

Yet even these are not rich enough for thy glory. We would sing unto thee a new song. We will, when we reach the heavenly shore, become leaders of the eternal music. 'Day without night' will we 'circle God's throne rejoicing', and count it the fullness of our glory, our bliss, our heaven, to wave the palm and cast our crowns with our songs at thy feet for ever and ever!

Our Father, which art in heaven, next to this we would offer prayer for those who never think of thee; who, though created by thee, are strangers to thee; who are fed by thy bounty, and yet never lift their voices to thee, but live for self, for the world, for Satan, for sin. Father, these cannot pray for themselves for they are dead; thy quickened children pray for them. These will not come to thee, for, like sheep, they are lost; but do thou seek them, Father, and bring them back.

Oh! our glorious Lord, thou hast taught us to pray for others, for the grace which could have met with such undeserving sinners as we are must be able to meet with the vilest of the vile. Oh! that we cannot boast of what we are; we cannot boast of what we have been by nature. Had we our doom we had now been in hell. Had we this day our proper, natural, and deserved position, we should still have been in the gall of bitterness and in the bond of iniquity. 'Tis thy rich, free, sovereign, distinguishing grace which has brought us up out of the miry clay, and set our feet upon a rock. And shall we even refuse to pray for others? Shall we leave a stone unturned for their conversion? Shall we not weep for those who have no tears and cry for those who have no prayers? Father, we must and we will.

'Fain our pity would reclaim,
And snatch the fire-brands from the flame.'

There are those who are utterly careless about divine things. Wilt thou impress them! May some stray shot reach their conscience! Oh! that they may be led solemnly to consider their position and their latter end! May thoughts of death and of eternity dash like some mighty waves, irresistibly against their souls! Oh! may heaven's light shine into their conscience! May they begin to ask themselves where they are, and what they are, and may they be turned unto the Lord with full purpose of heart.

There are others who are concerned, but they are halting between two opinions. There are some that we love in the flesh who have not yet decided for God. Behold it trembles in the balance! Cast in thy cross, O Jesus, and turn the scale! Oh! Love irresistible, come forth, and carry by blessed storm the hearts which have not yet yielded to all the attacks of the law! Oh! that some who never could be melted, even by the furnace of Sinai, may be dissolved by the beams of love from the tearful eyes of Jesus!

Lord, Lord, if there be a heart that is saying, 'Now, behold I yield; lo! at thy feet rebellion's weapons I lay down, and cease to be thy foe, thou King of kings' - if there be one who is saying, 'I am willing to be espoused unto Christ, to be washed in his blood, to be called in his righteousness' - bring that willing sinner in now! May there be no longer delay, but may this be the time when, once for all, the great transaction shall be done, and they shall be their Lord's and he shall be theirs.

Oh! that we could pour out our soul in prayer for the unconverted! Thou knowest where they will be in a few years! Oh! by thy wrath, we pray thee, let them not endure it! By the flames of hell be pleased to ransom them from going down into the pit! By everything that is dreadful in the wrath to come we do argue with thee to have mercy upon these sons of men, even upon those who have no mercy upon themselves. Father, hast thou not promised thy Son to see of his soul's travail? We point thee to the ransom paid; we point thee once again to the groans of thy Son, to his agony, and bloody sweat! Turn, turn thy glorious eyes thither, and then look on sinners, and speak the word, and bid them live.

Righteous Father, refresh every corner of the vineyard, and on every branch of the vine let the dew of heaven rest. Oh! that thou wouldest bless thy church throughout the world! Let visible union be established, or if not that, yet let the invisible union which has always existed be better recognised by believers. Wilt thou repair our schisms; wilt thou repair the breaches which have been made in the walls of Zion? Oh! that thou wouldest purge us of everything unscriptural, till all Christians shall come to the law and to the testimony, and still keep the ordinances and the doctrines as they were committed to the apostles by Christ!

Remember our land in this time of need. Do thou be pleased by some means to relieve the distress prevalent. Quicken the wheels of commerce that the many who are out of employment in this city may no longer be crying for work and bread. Oh! that thou wouldest make wars to cease to the ends of the earth, or, when they break out break thou the slave's fetters thereby, and though desperate be the evil, yet grant that Satan may cast out Satan, and may his kingdom be divided, and so fall.

Above all, thou long-expected Messiah, do thou come! Thine ancient people who despised thee once are waiting for thee in thy second coming, and we, the Gentiles, who knew thee not, neither regarded thee, we, too, are watching for thine advent. Make no tarrying, O Jesus! May thy feet soon stand again on Olivet! Thou shalt not have this time there to sweat great drops of blood, but thou shalt come to proclaim the year of vengeance for thy foes, and the year of acceptance for thy people.

> When wilt thou the heavens rend,
> In majesty come down?

Earth travails for thy coming. The whole creation groaneth in pain together until now. Thine own expect thee; we are longing till we are weary for thy coming. Come quickly, Lord Jesus, come quickly. Amen and Amen.

PRAYER 5

To the King Eternal

Our God and Father, draw us to thyself by thy Spirit, and may the few minutes that we spend in prayer be full of the true spirit of supplication. Grant that none of us with closed eyes may yet be looking abroad over the fields of vanity, but may our eyes be really shut to everything else now but that which is spiritual and divine. May we have communion with God in the secret of our hearts, and find him to be to us as a little sanctuary.

O Lord, we do not find it easy to get rid of distracting thoughts, but we pray thee help us to draw the sword against them and drive them away, and as when the birds came down upon his sacrifice Abraham drove them away, so may we chase away all cares, all thoughts of pleasure, everything else, whether it be pleasing or painful, that would keep us away from real fellowship with the Father and with his Son Jesus Christ.

We would begin with adoration. We worship from our hearts the Three in One, the infinitely glorious Jehovah, the only living and true God. We adore the Father, the Son and the Holy Ghost, the God of Abraham, of Isaac, and of Jacob. We are not yet ascended to the place where pure spirits behold the face of God, but we shall soon be there, perhaps much sooner than we think, and we would be there in spirit now, casting our crowns upon the glassy sea before the throne of the Infinite

Majesty, and ascribing glory and honour, and power and praise, and dominion and might to him that sitteth upon the throne, and unto the Lamb for ever and ever.

All the church doth worship thee, O God, every heart renewed by grace takes a delight in adoring thee, and we, among the rest, though least and meanest of them all, yet would bow as heartily as any worshipping, loving, praising, in our soul, being silent unto God because our joy in him is altogether inexpressible.

Lord, help us to worship thee in life as well as lip. May our whole being be taken up with thee. As when the fire fell down on Elijah's sacrifice of old and licked up even the water that was in the trenches, so may the consuming fire of the divine Spirit use up all our nature, and even that which might seem to hinder, even out of that may God get glory by the removal of it. Thus would we adore.

But, oh! dear Saviour, we come to thee, and we remember what our state is, and the condition we are in encourages us to come to thee now as beggars, as dependants upon thy heavenly charity. Thou art a Saviour, and as such thou art on the outlook for those that need saving, and here we are, here we come. We are the men and women thou art looking for, needing a Saviour.

Great Physician, we bring thee our wounds and bruises and putrefying sores, and the more diseased we are and the more conscious we are today of the depravity of our nature, of the deep-seated corruption of our hearts, the more we feel that we are the sort of beings that thou art seeking for, for the whole have no need of a physician but they that are sick.

Glorious Benefactor, we can meet thee on good terms, for we are full of poverty, we are just as empty as we can be. We could not be more abjectly dependent than we are. Since thou wouldest display thy mercy, here is our sin; since thou wouldest show thy strength, here is our weakness; since thou wouldest manifest thy loving-kindness, here are our needs; since thou wouldest glorify thy grace, here are we, such persons as can never have a shadow of a hope except through thy grace, for we are undeserving, ill-deserving, hell-deserving, and if thou do not magnify thy grace in us we must perish for ever.

And somehow we feel it sweet to come to thee in this way. If we had to tell thee that we had some good thing in us which thou didst require of us, we should be questioning whether we were not flattering ourselves and presumptuously thinking that we were better than we were. Lord Jesus, we come just as we are; this is how we came at first, and this is how we come still, with all our failures, with all our transgressions, with all and everything that is what it ought not to be, we come to thee. We do bless thee that thou dost receive us and our wounds, and by thy stripes we are healed; thou dost receive us and our sins, and by thy sin-bearing we are set clear and free from sin. Thou dost receive us and our death, even our death, for thou art he that liveth and was dead, and art alive for evermore.

We just come and lie at thy feet, obedient to that call of thine, 'Come unto me all ye that labour and I will give you rest'. Let us feel sweet rest, since we do come at thy call. May some come that have never come till this day, and may others who have been coming these many years consciously come again, coming unto thee as unto a living stone, chosen of God and precious, to build our everlasting hopes upon.

But, Lord, now that we are come so near thee, and on right terms with thee, we venture to ask thee this, that we that love thee may love thee very much more. Oh! since thou hast been precious, thy very name has music in it to our ears, and there are times when thy love is so inexpressibly strong upon us that we are carried away with it. We have felt that we would gladly die to increase thy honour. We have been willing to lose our name and our repute if so be thou mightest be glorified, and truly we often feel that if the crushing of us would lift thee one inch the higher, we would gladly suffer it.

For oh! thou blessed King, we would set the crown on thy head, even if the sword should smite our arm off at the shoulder blade. Thou must be King whatever becomes of us; thou must be glorified whatever becomes of us.

But yet we have to mourn that we cannot get always to feel as we should this rapture and ardour of love. Oh! at times thou dost manifest thyself to us so charmingly that heaven itself could scarce be happier than the world becomes when thou art with us in it. But when thou art gone and we are in the dark, oh! give us the love that loves in the dark, that loves when there is no comfortable sense of thy presence. Let us not be dependent upon feeling, but may we ever love thee, so that if thou didst turn thy back on us by the year together we would think none the less of thee, for thou art unspeakably to be beloved whatsoever thou doest, and if thou dost give us rough words, yet still we would cling to thee, and if the rod be used till we tingle again, yet still will we love thee, for thou art infinitely to be beloved of all men and angels, and thy Father loved thee. Make our hearts to love thee evermore the same. With all the capacity for love that there is in us, and with all the more that thou canst give us, may we love our Lord in spirit and in truth.

Help us, Lord, to conquer sin out of love to thee. Help some dear stragglers that have been mastered by sin sometimes, and they are struggling against it; give them the victory, Lord, and when the battle gets very sharp, and they are tempted to give way a little, help them to be very firm and very strong, never giving up hope in the Lord Jesus, and resolving that if they perish they will perish at his feet and nowhere else but there.

Lord, raise up in our churches many men and women that are all on fire with love to Christ and his divine gospel. Oh! give us back again men like Antipas, thy faithful martyr, men like Paul, thy earnest servant who proclaimed thy truth so boldly. Give us Johns, men to whom the Spirit may speak, who shall bid us hear what the Spirit saith unto the churches. Lord, revive us! Lord, revive us; revive thy work in the midst of the years in all the churches. Return unto the church of God in this country, return unto her. Thine adversaries think to have it all their own way, but they will not, for the Lord liveth, and blessed be our Rock.

Because of truth and righteousness, we beseech thee lay bare thine arm in these last days. O Shepherd of Israel, deal a heavy blow at the wolves and keep thy sheep in their own true pastures, free from the poisonous pastures of error. O God we would stir thee up. We know thou sleepest not, and yet sometimes it seems as if thou didst sleep awhile and leave things to go on in their own way.

We beseech thee awake. Plead thine own cause. We know thine answer, 'Awake! awake! put on thy strength, O Zion'. This we would do, Lord, but we cannot do it unless thou dost put forth thy strength to turn our weakness into might.

Great God, save this nation! O God of heaven and earth, stay the floods of infidelity and of filthiness that roll over this land. Would God we might see better days! Men seem entirely indifferent now. They will not come to hear the Word as once they did. God of our fathers, let thy Spirit work again among the masses. Turn the hearts of the people to the hearing of the Word, and convert them when they hear it. May it be preached with the Holy Ghost sent down from heaven.

Our hearts are weary for thee, thou King, thou King forgotten in thine own land, thou King despised among thine own people, when wilt thou yet be glorious before the eyes of all mankind? Come, we beseech thee, come quickly, or if thou comest not personally, send forth the Holy Spirit with a greater power than ever that our hearts may leap within us as they see miracles of mercy repeated in our midst.

Father, glorify thy Son. Somehow our prayer always comes to this before we have done. 'Father, glorify thy Son that thy Son also may glorify thee', and let the days comes when he shall see of the travail of his soul and shall be satisfied. Bless all work done for thee, whether it be in the barn or in the cathedral, silently and quietly in the street door, or in the Sunday-school, or in the classes, O Lord, bless thy work. Hear also prayers that have been put up by wives for their husbands, children for their parents, parents for their children. Let the holy service of prayer never cease, and let the intercession be accepted of God, for Jesus Christ's sake. Amen.

PRAYER 6

The Wonders of Calvary

Great God, there was a time when we dreaded the thought of coming near to thee, for we were guilty and thou wast angry with us, but now we will praise thee because thine anger is turned away, and thou comfortest us. Ay, and the very throne which once was a place of dread has now become the place of shelter. I flee unto thee to hide me.

We long now to get right away from the world, even from the remembrance of it, and have fellowship with the world to come by speaking with him that was, and is, and is to come, the Almighty. Lord, we have been worried and wearied oftentimes with care, but with thee care comes to an end, all things are with thee, and when we live in thee we live in wealth, in sure repose, in constant joy.

We have to battle with the sons of men against a thousand errors and unrighteousnesses, but when we flee to thee, there all is truth and purity and holiness, and our heart finds peace. Above all, we have to battle with ourselves, and we are very much ashamed of ourselves. After many years of great mercy, after tasting of the powers of the world to come, we still are so weak, so foolish; but, oh! when we get away from self to God there all is truth and purity and holiness, and our heart finds peace, wisdom, completeness, delight, joy, victory.

Oh! bring us, then, we pray thee, now near to thyself. Let

us bathe ourselves in communion with our God. Blessed be the love which chose us before the world began. We can never sufficiently adore thee for thy sovereignty, the sovereignty of love which saw us in the ruins of the Fall, yet loved us notwithstanding all.

We praise the God of the Eternal Council Chamber and of the everlasting covenant, but where shall we find sufficiently fit words with which to praise him who gave us grace in Christ his Son, before he spread the starry sky.

We also bless thee, O God, as the God of our redemption, for thou hast so loved us as to give even thy dear Son for us. He gave himself, his very life for us that he might redeem us from all iniquity and separate us unto himself to be his peculiar people, zealous for good works.

Never can we sufficiently adore free grace and dying love. The wonders of Calvary never cease to be wonders, they are growingly marvellous in our esteem as we think of him who washed us from our sins in his own blood. Nor can we cease to praise the God of our regeneration who found us dead and made us live, found us at enmity and reconciled us, found us loving the things of this world and lifted us out of the slough and mire of selfishness and worldliness into the love of divine everlasting things.

O Spirit of God, we love thee this day, especially for dwelling in us. How canst thou abide in so rude a habitation. How canst thou make these bodies to be thy temples, and yet thou dost so, for which let thy name be had in reverence so long as we live.

O Lord, we would delight ourselves in thee this day. Give us faith and love and hope that with these three graces we may draw very near to the Triune God. Thou wilt keep us, thou wilt preserve us, thou wilt feed us, thou wilt lead us, and thou wilt bring us to the mind of God, and there wilt thou show us thy love, and in the glory everlasting and boundless, there wilt thou make us know and taste and feel the joys that cannot be expressed.

But a little longer waiting and we shall come to the golden shore; but a little longer fighting and we shall receive the crown of life that fadeth not away.

Lord, get us up above the world. Come, Holy Spirit, heavenly Dove, and mount and bear us on thy wings, far from these inferior sorrows and inferior joys, up where eternal ages roll. May we ascend in joyful contemplation, and may our spirit come back again, strong for all its service, armed for all its battles, armoured for all its dangers, and made ready to live heaven on earth, until by and by we shall live heaven in heaven.

Great Father, be with thy waiting people, any in great trouble do thou greatly help; any that are despondent do thou sweetly comfort and cheer; any that have erred, and are smarting under their own sin, do thou bring them back and heal their wounds; any that this day are panting after holiness do thou give them the desire of their hearts; any that are longing for usefulness do thou lead them into ways of usefulness.

Lord, we want to live while we live. We do pray that we may not merely groan out an existence here below, nor live as earthworms crawling back into our holes and dragging now and then a sere leaf with us; but oh! give us to live as we ought to live, with a new life that thou hast put into us, with the divine quickening which has lifted us as much above common men as men are lifted above the beasts that perish.

Do not let us always be hampered like poor half-hatched birds within the egg; may we chip the shell today and get out into the glorious liberty of the children of God. Grant us this, we pray thee.

Lord, visit our church. We have heard thy message to the churches at Ephesus; it is a message to us also. Oh! do not let any of us lose our first love. Let not our church grow cold and dead. We are not, we fear, what once we were. Lord, revive us! All our help must come from thee. Give back to the church its love, its confidence, its holy daring, its consecration, its liberality, its holiness. Give back all it ever had and give it much more. Take every member and wash his feet, sweet Lord, most tenderly, and set us with clean feet in a clean road, with a clean heart to guide them, and do thou bless us as thou art wont to do after a divine fashion.

Bless us, our Father, and let all the churches of Jesus Christ partake of like care and tenderness. Walking among the golden candlesticks, trim every lamp and make every light, even though it burneth but feebly now, to shine out gloriously through thy care.

Now bless the sinners. Lord, convert them. O God, save men, save this great city, this wicked city, this slumbering dead city. Lord, arouse it, arouse it by any means, that it may turn unto its God. Lord, save sinners all the world over, and let thy precious Word be fulfilled. 'Behold He cometh with clouds.' Why dost thou tarry? Make no tarrying, O our Lord. And now unto Father, Son and Holy Ghost be glory forever and ever. Amen.

PRAYER 7

'Let all the people praise thee'

Our Father, when we read thy description of human nature we are sure it is true, for thou hast seen man ever since his fall, and thou hast been grieved at heart concerning him. Moreover, thou hast such a love towards him that thou didst not judge him harshly; and every word that thou hast spoken must be according to truth. Thou hast measured and computed the iniquity of man, for thou hast laid it on the Well-Beloved; and we know thou hast not laid upon him more than is meet.

O God, we are distressed, we are bowed down greatly when we see what is the condition to which we and all our race have fallen. 'Where is boasting then?' And yet we grieve to say that we do boast, and have boasted; and that our fellow men are great at boasting; whereas they ought rather to lay their hands upon their mouths before thee.

It has become a wonder to us that thou shouldst look upon man at all; the most hateful object in creation must be a man, because he slew thy Son, because he has multiplied rebellions against a just and holy law. And yet truly there is no sight that gives thee more pleasure than man, for Jesus was a man; and the brightness of his glory covers all our shame, and the pureness and perfectness of his obedience shine like the sun in the midst of the thick darkness. For his sake thou art well pleased, and thou dost dwell with us.

Lord, we once thought that those descriptions of our heart were somewhat strained, but we think not so now, for verily we perceive that had it not been for restraint which held us like fetters we, in our unregenerate state, were capable of anything; for, even now, when we are regenerate, the old sin that abideth in us is capable of reaching to a high degree of infamy; and did not the new life restrain the old death we know not what we might yet become.

We thought once we were humble, but we soon found that our pride will feed on any current flattery that is laid at our door. We thought we were believers, but sometimes we are so doubting, so unbelieving, so vexed with scepticism that we should not certainly choose to follow: that is thy work in us. By nature we are such liars that we think thee a liar too; the surest token of our untruthfulness, that we think that thou canst be untrue.

Oh, this base heart of ours! Hath it not enough tinder in it to set on fire the course of nature? If a spark do but fall into it, any one of our members left to itself would dishonour Christ, deny the Lord that bought us, and turn back into perdition.

We are altogether ashamed. Truly in us is fulfilled thine own Word: 'Thou shalt be a shame, and never open thy mouth any more'. For thy love to us hath silenced us, that great love hath hidden boasting from us; thy great love, wherewith thou lovedst us even when we were dead in trespasses and sins; thy great love wherewith thou hast loved us still, despite our ill manners, our wanderings, our shortcomings, and our excesses.

Oh, the matchless love of God! Truly if there be any glory it must be all the Lord's; if there be any virtue it is the result of grace; if there be anything whatsoever that lifts us above the devil himself it is the work of the divine Spirit, to whom be glory!

And now at the remembrance of all this, and being in thy presence, we do yet rejoice that covered is our unrighteousness; from condemnation we are free, and we are the favoured of the Lord. Thou hast given us, O Lord, to taste of that love which is not merely laid up for us, but we have enjoyed it, and do enjoy it still.

Our heart knows the Father's love, for we have received the spirit of adoption, whereby we cry, 'Abba, Father'. And we joy and rejoice in the redemption of our spirits, and we expect the redemption of our bodies, when, at the coming of the Lord they too shall be raised incorruptible, and we shall be changed.

O Jesus, thou wilt bring thy Israel out of Egypt, and not a hoof shall be left behind; no, not a bone, nor a piece of thine elect shall be left in the hands of the adversary. We shall come out clean, delivered by him who doeth nothing by halves, but who on the cross said, 'It is finished'. Who much more will say it on his throne.

Glory be unto Father, Son and Holy Ghost, who hath lifted us up from our ruin and condemnation, and made us new creatures, and justified us, and guaranteed us eternal life, which eternal life shall be manifested at the coming of the Lord. All glory be unto his ever blessed name forever and ever!

And now, Lord, during the few days that remain to us here below, be it all our business to cry, 'Behold the Lamb!' Oh! teach these hearts to be always conscious of thy love; and then these lips, that they may set out as best they can by thy divine help the matchless story of the cross. Oh! do give us to win many to Jesus, let us not be barren, but may we have to cry that we are the beloved of the Lord, and our offspring with us. May we have many spiritual offspring that shall go with us to the throne, that we may say before him, 'I and the children that thou hast given me'.

Lord, bless the work of the church and all its branches; and let thy kingdom come into the hearts of multitudes by its means. Remember all churches that are really at work for Jesus, and all private individuals, workers alone, workers by themselves. Let the Lord's own name be made known by tens of thousands. Give the Word, and great may be the multitude of them that publish it. Let all this, our beloved country, know Christ, and come to his feet; let the dark places of this huge city be enlightened with the sweet name of Jesus. And then let the heathen know thee, and the uttermost part of the earth hear of thee.

Oh! from the tree declare thou thy salvation, and from the throne let it be published in proclamations of a king. 'Let the people praise thee, O God; yea, let all the people praise thee'.

Our heart seems as if it had not anything else to ask for when it reaches to this; yet would we go back a moment and say: Lord, forgive us our sins; Lord, sanctify our persons; Lord, guide us in difficulty; Lord, supply our needs. The Lord teach us; the Lord perfect us; the Lord comfort us; the Lord make us meet for the appearing of his Son from heaven!

And now we come back to a theme that still seems to engross our desires. Oh! that Christ might come. Oh! that his Word might be made known to the uttermost ends of the earth! Lord, they die, they perish, they pass away by multitudes! Every time the sun rises and sets they pass away! Make no tarrying, we beseech thee. Give wings to the feet of thy messengers, and fire to their mouths, that they may proclaim the Word with Pentecostal swiftness and might. Oh! that thy kingdom might come, and thy will be done on earth as it is in heaven, for thine is the kingdom, the power and the glory, for ever and ever. Amen.

PRAYER 8

A Prayer for Holiness

Our Father, we worship and love thee; and it is one point of our worship that thou art holy. Time was when we loved thee for thy mercy; we knew no more; but now thou hast changed our hearts and made us in love with goodness, purity, justice, true holiness; and we understand now why 'the cherubim and seraphim continually do cry, Holy, Holy, Lord God of hosts'.

We adore thee because thou art holy, and we love thee for thine infinite perfection. For now we sigh and cry after holiness ourselves. Sanctify us wholly, spirit, soul and body. Lord, we mourn over the sins of our past life and our present shortcomings. We bless thee thou hast forgiven us; we are reconciled to thee by the death of thy Son. There are many who know that they have been washed, and that he that beareth away sin has borne their sin away. These are they who now cry to thee to be delivered from the power of sin, to be delivered from the power of temptation without, but especially from indwelling sin within.

Lord, purify us in head, heart and hand; and if it be needful that we should be put into the fire to be refined as silver is refined, we would even welcome the fire if we may be rid of the dross. Lord, save us from constitutional sin, from sins of temperament, from sins of our surroundings. Save us from ourselves in every shape, and grant us especially to have the light of love strong within us.

May we love God; may we love thee, O Saviour; may we love the people of God as being members of one body in connection with thee. May we love the guilty world with that love which desires its salvation and conversion; and may we love not in word only, but in deed and in truth. May we help the helpless, comfort the mourner, sympathise with the widow and fatherless, and may we be always ready to put up with wrong, to be long suffering, to be very patient, full of forgiveness, counting it a small thing that we should forgive our fellow men since we have been forgiven of God. Lord, tune our hearts to love, and then give us an inward peace, a restfulness about everything.

May we have no burden to carry, because, though we have a burden, we have rolled it upon the Lord. May we take up our cross, and because Christ has once died on the cross may our cross become a comfort to us. May we count it all joy when we fall into divers trials, knowing that in all this God will be glorified, his image will be stamped upon us, and the eternal purpose will be fulfilled, wherein he has predestinated us to be conformed unto the image of his Son.

Lord, look upon thy people. We might pray about our troubles. We will not; we will only pray against our sins. We might come to thee about our weariness, about our sickness, about our disappointment, about our poverty; but we will leave all that, we will only come about sin. Lord, make us holy, and then do what thou wilt with us.

We pray thee, help us to adorn the doctrine of God our Saviour in all things. If we are fighting against sin - 'the sin which doth so easily beset us' - Lord, lend us heavenly weapons and heavenly strength that we may cut the giants down, these men of Anak that come against us. We feel very feeble. Oh! make us strong in the Lord, in the power of his might. May we never let sin have any rest in us, may we chase it, drive it out, slay it, hang it on a tree, abhor it, and may we 'cleave to that which is good'.

Some of us are trying, striving after some excellent virtue. Lord, help strugglers; enable those that contend against great difficulties only to greater grace, more faith, and so to bring them nearer to God. Lord, we will be holy; by thy grace we will never rest until we are. Thou hast begun a good work in us and thou wilt carry it on. Thou wilt work in us to will and to do of thine own good pleasure.

Lord, help the converted child to be correct in his relation to his parents; help the Christian father or mother to be right in dealing with children, 'may they not provoke their children to anger lest they may discourage'. Take away wilfulness from the young; take away impatience from the old. Lord, help Christian men of business. May they act uprightly; may Christian masters never be hard to their servants, to their workpeople; and may Christian workpeople give to their masters that which is just and equal in the way of work in return for wage. May we as Christian men be always standing upon our rights, but always be willing each one to minister to the help of others.

And, oh that as Christians we might be humble! Lord, take away that stiff-necked, that proud look; take away from us the spirit of 'stand by, for I am holier than thou'; make us condescend to men of low estate; ay, and even to men of low morals, low character. May we seek them out, seek their good. Oh! give to the church of Christ an intense love for the souls of men. May it make our hearts break to think that they will perish in their sin. May we grieve every day because of the sin of this city. Set a mark upon our forehead and let us be known to thyself as men that sigh and cry for all the abominations that are done in the midst of the city.

O God, save us from a hard heart, an unkind spirit, that is insensible to the woes of others. Lord, preserve thy people also from worldliness, from rioting, from drunkenness, from chambering and wantonness, from strife and envy, from everything that would dishonour the name of Christ that we bear. Lord, make us holy. Our prayer comes back to this. Make us holy; cleanse the inside and let the outside be clean too. Make us holy, O God: do this for Christ's sake. Not that we hope to be saved by our own holiness, but that holiness is salvation. Then we are saved from sin. Lord, help thy poor children to be holy. Oh! keep us so if we are so; keep us even from stumbling, and present us faultless before thy presence at last.

We pray for friends that are ill, for many that are troubled because of the illness of others. We bring before thee every case of trouble and trial known to us, and ask for thy gracious intervention. We pray for thy ministers everywhere; for thy missionary servants. Remember brethren that are making great sacrifice out in the hot sun or in the cold and frozen north. Everywhere preserve those who for Christ's sake carry their lives in their hands.

And our brethren at home, in poverty many of them, working for Christ, Lord, accept them and help us to help them. Sunday-school teachers, do thou remember them; and the tract visitors from door to door, and the city missionaries, and the Bible women, all who in any way endeavour to bring Christ under the notice of men. O, help them all.

We will offer but one more prayer, and it is this. Lord, look in pity upon any who are not in Christ. May they be converted. May they pass from death to life, and they will never forget it; may they see the eternal light for the first time, and they will remember it even in eternity. Father, help us; bless us now for Jesu's sake. Amen.

PRAYER 9

Glorious Liberty

Our Father, we bless thy name that we can say from the bottom of our hearts, 'Abba, Father'. It is the chief joy of our lives that we have become the children of God by faith which is in Christ Jesus, and we can in the deep calm of our spirit say, 'Our Father, which art in heaven, hallowed be thy name; thy kingdom come; thy will be done in earth as in heaven'.

Lord, we thank thee for the liberty which comes to our emancipated spirit through the adoption which thou hast made us to enjoy. When we were in servitude the chains were heavy, for we could not keep thy law; there was an inward spirit of rebellion. When the commandment came it irritated our corrupt nature and sin revived, and we died.

Even when we had some strivings after better things, yet the power that was in us lusted unto evil, and the spirit of the Hagarene was upon us. We wanted to fly from the Father's house; we were wild men, men of the wilderness, and we loved not living in the Father's house.

O God, we thank thee that we have not been cast out. Indeed, if thou hadst then cast out the child of the bondwoman thou hadst cast us out, but now through sovereign grace all is altered with us. Blessed be thy name. It is a work of divine power and love over human nature, for now we are the children of the promise, certainly not born according to the strength of the human will, or of blood, or of birth, but born by the Holy Ghost through the power of the Word, begotten again unto a lively hope by the resurrection of Jesus Christ from the dead, children of the great Father who is in heaven, having his life within us. Now, like Isaac, we are heirs according to promise and heirs of the promise, and we dwell at home in the Father's house, and our soul is satisfied as with marrow and fatness, and our mouth shall praise thee as with joyful lips.

O God, we would not change places with angels, much less with kings of the earth. To be indeed thy sons and daughters - the thought of it doth bring to our soul a present heaven, and the fruition of it shall be our heaven, to dwell forever in the house of the Lord, and go no more out, but to be his sons and his heirs for ever and ever.

Our first prayer is for others who as yet are in bondage. We thank thee, Lord, that thou hast given them the spirit of bondage and made them to fear. We are glad that they should be brought to feel the evil of sin, to feel the perfection of thy law, to know something of the fiery nature of thy justice, and so to be shut up unto salvation by grace through faith. But, Lord, let them not tarry long under the pedagogue, but may the schoolmaster with his rod bring them to Christ.

Lord, cure any of thy chosen of self-righteousness; deliver them from any hope in their own abilities, but keep them low. Bring them out of any hope of salvation by their own prayers or their own repentance. Bring them to cast themselves upon thy grace to be saved by trusting in Christ. Emancipate them from all observance of days, weeks, months, years, and things of human institution, and bring them into the glorious liberty of the children of God that thy law may become their delight, thyself become their strength, their all, thy Son become their joy and their crown. We do pray this with all our hearts.

Lord, deliver any of thy children from quarrelling with thee. Help us to be always at one with our God. 'It is the Lord; let him do what seemeth him good', and blessed be his name for ever and ever.

God, bless our country, and the sister country across the flood, and all lands where thy name is known and reverenced, and heathen lands where it is unknown. God, bless the outposts, the first heralds of mercy, and everywhere may the Lord's kingdom come and his name be glorified. Glory be unto the Father, and to the Son, and to the Holy Ghost; as it was in the beginning, is now, and ever shall be, world without end. Amen.

PRAYER 10

The Music of Praise

O thou blessed God, we must be helped of thy Spirit or we cannot worship thee aright. Behold the holy angels adore thee, and the hosts redeemed by blood bring everlasting Hallelujahs to thy feet. What are we, the creatures of a day, polluted with sin, that we should think that we can praise thee? And yet the music of praise were not complete if thy children did not join in it, even those of them who are still in this world below. Help us, then; enable us to tune our harps and to fetch forth music from our spirit.

Verily, Lord, if there are any creatures in the world that can praise thee we ought to do so. Each one among us feels that he has some special reason for gratitude. Lord, it is an unspeakable mercy to know thee - to know thee as our reconciled God, to know thee as our Father in Christ Jesus, who has forgiven us all our trespasses. Oh! it is unspeakably sweet to come and rest in thee, and to know that there is now no cause of quarrel between us and thee; on the contrary, that we are bound to one another by a covenant which in infinite tenderness and mercy thou hast made, that thy people might have strong consolation, and might boldly take hold on thee.

Oh! the joy of knowing that we are thine forever, thine in the trials of life, and thine in the last dread of death, and then thine in resurrection, thine throughout eternity. We do therefore worship thee, O God, not as a constraining nor under terror or pressure, but cheerfully and gladly, ascribing unto thee praise, and power, and dominion, and glory, and honour, world without end.

We wish we knew how to do something for thee. We pray that we may be helped to do so ere we die; yea, that every flying hour may confess that we have brought thy gospel some renown; that we may so live as to extend the Redeemer's kingdom at least in some little measure; that ours may not be a fruitless, wasted life; that no faculty of ours may lay by and rust; but to the utmost of our capacity may we be helped of the divine Spirit to spend our whole life in real adoration.

We know that he prays that serves, he praises that gives, he adores that obeys, and the life is the best music. Oh! set it to good music, we pray thee, and help us all through to keep to each note, and may there be no false note in all the singing of our life, but all be according to that sacred score which is written out so fully in the life music of our Lord.

We beseech thee to look down upon thy children, and cheer us. Lord, lift us up. Come, Holy Spirit, like a fresh bracing wind, and let our spirit, through thy Spirit, rise upward towards God.

We would with much shamefacedness acknowledge our transgressions and sins. There are some that never felt the burden of sin at all. Lord, lay it on them; press them with it. Almighty God, vex their souls; let them find no rest till they find rest in thee. May they never be content to live and die in sin, but of thine infinite mercy come to them, and make them sorry for their sin.

As for thy people we are grieved to think that we do not live better than we do. Blessed be thy name for every fruit of holiness, for every work of faith, but oh! for more. Thou hast changed the tree; it is no longer a bramble; it can bring forth figs, but now we want to bring forth more of these sweet fruits.

The Lord make us to love Christ intensely, to love the souls of men most heartily, to love thy truth with earnestness, to love the name of Jesus above everything. May we be ravished with the sound of it. The Lord give us to have every grace, not only love, but faith, and hope, and holy gentleness, meekness, patience, brotherly love. Build us up, we pray thee, Lord, in all knowledge, and in all experience, and give us with this submission to thy will, holy resignation, great watchfulness, much carefulness in our speech, that we may rule the tongue, and so rule the whole body.

The Lord pour out his Spirit upon us that every chamber of our nature may be sweetened and perfumed with the indwelling of God, till our imagination shall only delight in things chaste and pure; till our memory shall cast out the vile stuff from the dark chambers; till we shall expect and long for heavenly things, and our treasure shall all be in heaven and our heart be there. Take our highest manhood, Lord, and saturate it in thy love, till like Gideon's fleece it is filled with dew, every lock and every single fleck of it, not a single portion of it left unmoistened by the dew from heaven.

How do we bless thee for many that are striving to walk as Christ walked, and who are also trying to bring others to Christ. O Lord, help us in this struggle after holiness and usefulness; and as thou hast given to many the desire of their hearts in this respect up to a certain measure, now enlarge their hearts, and give them more both of holiness and usefulness. Oh! give us to be like trees planted by the rivers of water, that we ourselves may be vigorous, and then give us to bring forth abundant fruit according to our season, to the praise and glory of God.

Our desire is that we may be quickened in our progress towards the celestial life. Visit us with thy salvation. Lord, let us not only have life, but let us have it more abundantly. May we every one of us quicken his pace, and may we run more earnestly than ever towards the mark that is set before us.

Remember all thy church throughout the whole world. Prosper missionary operations. Be with any ministers or missionaries that are depressed for lack of success. Be with any that are rejoicing because of success. May each heart be kept in a right state, so that thou mayest use thy servants to the utmost of possibility.

O God, send us better days than these, we pray thee. We thank thee for all the light there is, but send us more light. We thank thee for what life there is among Christians, but send more of it. Bind the churches together in unity, and then give them such speed, such force, such power that they shall break into the ranks of the adversary, and the victory shall be unto Christ and to his people.

Remember our dear country. Bless the Sovereign. Remember all those that lead our legislature. Be gracious unto all ranks and conditions of men. Have mercy upon all that are poor and needy, all that are sick and sorrowing, and that are tossed upon the sea. Remember the prisoners and such as have no helper. Be gracious to such as are in the article of death. And, finally, let the day come when the Sun shall shine forth in all his brightness, even Christ Jesus shall be manifested, to be admired in them that believe, and to make glad the whole creation. Make no tarrying, O thou Sun of Righteousness, but come forth speedily. We ask it for thy name's sake. Amen.

PRAYER 11

Under the Blood

Jehovah our God, we thank thee for leaving on record the story of thine ancient people. It is full of instruction to ourselves. Help us to take its warning to avoid the faults into which they fell! Thou art a covenant God, and thou keepest thy promises and thy Word never faileth. We have proved this so hitherto:

> 'Thus far we find that promise good,
> Which Jesus ratified with blood.'

But as for ourselves we are like Israel of old, a fickle people, and, we confess it with great shame, there are days when we take the timbrel and sing with Miriam 'unto the Lord who triumphed gloriously', and yet, we grieve to say it, not many hours after, we are thirsty, and we cry for water, and we murmur in our tents; the brackish Marah turns our heart and we are grieved with our God. Sometimes we bow before thee with reverence and awe when we behold thy Sinai altogether on a smoke; but there have been times when we have set up the golden calf and we have said of some earthly things, 'These be thy gods, O Israel'. We believe with intensity of faith and then doubt with a horribleness of doubt.

Lord, thou hast been very patient with us. Many have been our provocations, many have been thy chastisements, but:

'Thy strokes are fewer than our crimes,
And lighter than our guilt.'

'Thou hast not dealt with us after our sins, nor rewarded us according to our iniquities.' Blessed be thy name!

And now fulfil that part of the covenant wherein thou hast said, 'A new heart also will I give thee and a right spirit will I put within thee. I will put my fear in their hearts and they shall not depart from me.' Hold us fast and then we shall hold fast to thee. Turn us and we shall be turned, keep us and we shall keep thy statutes.

We cry to thee that we may no more provoke thee. We beg thee rather to send the serpents among us than to let sin come among us. Oh! that we might have our eye always on the brazen serpent that healeth all the bites of evil, but may we not look to sin nor love it. Let not the devices of Balaam and of Balak prevail against us, to lead thy people away from their purity. Let us not be defiled with false doctrine or with unholy living, but may we walk as the separated people of God and keep ourselves unspotted from the world. Lord, we would not grieve thy Spirit. Oh! may we never vex thee so as to lead thee in thy wrath to say, 'They shall not enter into my rest'. Bear with us still for his dear sake whose blood is upon us. Bear with us still and send not the destroying angel as thou didst to Egypt, but again fulfil that promise of thine, 'When I see the blood I will pass over you'.

Just now may we be consciously passed over by the Spirit of condemnation; may we know in our hearts that 'there is therefore now no condemnation to them that are in Christ Jesus'. May we feel the peace-giving power of the divine absolution. May we come into thy holy presence with our feet washed in the brazen laver, hearing our great High Priest say to us, 'Ye are clean every whit'. Thus made clean may we draw near to God through Jesus Christ our Lord.

Further, our heavenly Father, we come before thee now washed in the blood, wearing the snow-white robe of Christ's righteousness, and we ask thee to remember thy people. Some are sore burdened; lighten the burden or strengthen the shoulder. Some are bowed down with fear; peradventure they mistrust; forgive the mistrust and give a great increase of faith that they may trust thee where they cannot trace thee. The Lord remember any who bear the burden of others. Some cry to thee day and night about the sins of the times, about the wanderings of thy church. Lord hear our prayers! We would bear this yoke for thee, but help us to bear it without fearing so as to distrust thee. May we know that thou wilt take care of thine own cause and preserve thine own truth, and may we therefore be restful about it all.

Some are crying to thee for the conversion of relatives and friends; this burden they have taken up to follow after Jesus in the cross bearing. Grant them to see the desire of their heart fulfilled. God save our children and children's children, and if we have unconverted relatives of any kind, the Lord have mercy upon them for Christ's sake. Give us joy in them - as much joy in them as Christians as we have had sorrow about them as unbelievers.

Further, be pleased to visit thy church with the Holy Spirit. Renew the day of Pentecost in our midst, and in the midst of all gatherings of thy people may there come the downfall of the holy fire, the uprising of the heavenly wind. May matters that are now slow and dead become quick and full of life, and may the Lord Jesus Christ be exalted in the midst of his church which is his fullness, 'the fullness of him that filleth all in all'. May multitudes be converted; may they come flocking to Christ with holy eagerness to find in him a refuge as the doves fly to their dove-cotes.

Oh! for salvation work throughout these islands and across the sea and in every part of the world, specially in heathen lands. Bring many to Christ's feet, we pray thee, everywhere where men are ready to lay down their lives that they may impart the heavenly life of Christ. Work, Lord, work mightily! Thy church cries to thee. Oh, leave us not! We can do nothing without thee! Our strength is wholly thine! Come to us with great power, and let thy Word have free course and be glorified.

Remember every one that calls thee Father. May a Father's love look on all the children. May the special need of each one be supplied, the special sorrow of each one be assuaged. May we be growing Christians, may we be working Christians, may we be perfected Christians, may we come to the fullness of the stature of men in Christ Jesus. Lord Jesus, thou art a great pillar; in thee doth all fullness dwell. Thou didst begin thy life with filling the waterpots to the full; thou didst fill Simon Peter's boat until it began to sink; thou didst fill the house where thy people were met together with the presence of the Holy Ghost; thou dost fill heaven; thou wilt surely fill all things; fill us, oh! fill us today with all the fullness of God, and make thy people thus joyful and strong, and gracious and heavenly!

But we cannot leave off our prayer when we have prayed for thy people, though we have asked large things; we want thee to look among the thousands and millions round about us who know thee not. Lord, look on the masses who go nowhere to worship. Have pity upon them; Father, forgive them, for they know not what they do. Give a desire to hear thy Word. Send upon the people some desire after their God. O Lord, take sinners in hand thyself. Oh! come and reach obstinate, obdurate minds; let the careless and the frivolous begin to think upon eternal things. May there be an uneasiness of heart, a sticking of the arrows of God in their loins, and may they seek too the great Physician and find healing this very day. Ah! Lord, thou sayest, 'Today, if ye will hear his voice', and we take up the echo. Save men today, even today. Bring them thy Spirit in power that they may be willing to rest in Christ. Lord, hear, forgive, accept and bless, for Jesu's sake. Amen.

PRAYER 12

On Holy Ground

'Our Father, which art in heaven, hallowed be thy name, thy kingdom come, thy will be done on earth as it is in heaven.' We fear that we often begin our prayer with petitions for ourselves, and put our daily bread before thy kingdom, and the pardoning of our sins before the hallowing of thy name. We would not do so today, but guided by our Lord's model of prayer, we would first pray for thy glory, and here, great God, we would adore thee. Thou hast made us and not we ourselves. We are thy people, and the sheep of thy pasture. All glory be unto thee, Jehovah, the only living and true God.

With heart and mind, and memory and fear, and hope and joy, we worship the Most High. It well becomes us to put our shoes from off our feet when we draw near to God, for the place whereon we stand is holy ground. If God in the bush demanded the unsandalled foot of the prophet, how much more shall God in Christ Jesus?

With lowliest reverence, with truest love, we worship God in Christ Jesus, uniting therein with all the redeemed host above, with angels and principalities and powers. We cannot cast crowns at his feet, for we have none as yet, but if there be any virtue, if there be any praise, if there be about us anything of grace and good repute, we ascribe it all to God. We cannot veil our faces with our wings, for we have none, but we veil them with something better than angelic wings, the blood and righteousness of Jesus Christ. With these we cover our faces, with these we cover our feet, and with these we fly up to God in holiest fellowship of God. Glory, and honour, and power, and dominion be unto him that sitteth upon the throne, and unto the Lamb for ever and ever.

Great God, we long that thou mayest be known upon the ends of the earth, that the idols may be utterly abolished. We long that false doctrine may fly like birds of darkness before the light and thy coming. Reign thou in the hearts of our fellow men. Lord, subdue sin, and under thy feet let drunkenness, and unchastity, and oppression, and every form of wickedness be put away by the gospel of Jesus Christ and his Holy Spirit.

Oh! that today, even today, many hearts might be won to God. Convince men of the wrong of being alienated from God, put into their hearts sorrow for sin and dread of wrath to come and lead and drive men to Christ. Oh! how we pray for this, the salvation of our fellow men, not so much for their sakes as for the sake of the glory of God and the rewarding of Christ for his pain.

We do with all our hearts pray, 'Thy kingdom come, thy will be done on earth, as it is in heaven'. Lord, help us to do thy will. Take the crippled kingdom of our manhood and reign thou over it. Let spirit and body be consecrated to God. May there be no reserves; may everything be given up to thee. Reign forever! Pierced King, despised and nailed to a tree, sit thou on the glorious high throne in our hearts, and may our lives prove that thou art Lord over us; by our every thought and desire, and imagination, and word, and act, in every respect being under thy divine control.

Thy people breathe to thee out of their very hearts the prayer that thou mayest reign over us without a rival. O

Saviour, use for thyself what thou hast bought with blood, and drive out the enemy, and let no power have any dominion over us except the power of thy good Spirit which worketh righteousness and peace.

We pray today also that thy truth may prevail against the many antichrists that have gone forth against it. Our Father, restore a pure language to thy Zion once again. Take away, we pray thee, the itching for new doctrine, the longing for that which is thought to be scientific and wise above what is written, and may thy church come to her moorings, may she cast anchor in the truth of God and there abide; and if it be thy will may we live to see brighter and better times.

If it might be so we would pray for the coming of our Lord very speedily to end these sluggish years, these long delaying days. But, if he come not, yet put power into thy truth and quicken thy church that she may become energetic for the spread of it, that so thy kingdom may come. This do we seek first and above everything, the glory of God. We ask for grace that we may live with this end in view. May we lay ourselves out to it. May this be our morning thought, the thought that we have in our minds when we lay awake at nights. What shall I do, my Saviour, to praise? How can I make him illustrious and win another heart to his throne?

Now bless us; forgive us our trespasses wherein we have sinned against thee. Seal our pardon upon our consciences, and make us feel that as we truly forgive them that trespass against us, so hast thou forgiven us all our iniquities. We pray thee lead us not into temptation. Do not try us, Lord, nor suffer the devil to try us. If we must be tried then deliver us from evil, and especially from the evil one, that he may get no dominion over us.

Oh! keep us, Lord. This life is full of trial. There are many that are perplexed about temporary things. Let not the enemy lead them to do or think aught that is amiss, because of the straitness of supply. Others are blessed with prosperity. Lord, let it not be a curse to them. Let them know how to abound as well as to suffer loss. In all things may they be instructed to glorify God, not only with all they are, but with all they have, and even with all they have not, by a holy contentment to do without that which it doth not please thee to bestow.

And then, Lord, give us day by day our daily bread; provide for thy poor people; let them not think that the provision for themselves rests fully on themselves, but may they cry to thee, for thou hast said, 'Thy bread shall be given thee, thy waters shall be sure'. If we follow thee, if thou lead us into a desert, thou wilt strew our path with manna. May thy people believe this, and let them have no care, but like the birds of the air which neither sow nor gather into barns, and yet are fed, so may thy people be.

But, above all, give us spiritual help. Give us wisdom, which is profitable to get. Give us the absence of all self-seeking, and a complete yielding up of our desires to the will of God. Help us to be as Christ was, who was not his own, but gave himself to his Father for our sins; so may we for his sake give ourselves up to do or suffer the will of our Father who is in heaven.

Remember thy people in their families and convert their children; give us help and strength; spare precious lives that are in danger; be gracious to any that are dying; may the life of God swallow up the death of the body. Prepare us all for thy glorious advent; keep us waiting and watching, and do thou come quickly to our heart's desire, for we pray, 'Thy kingdom come, thy will be done on earth, as it is in heaven, for thine is the kingdom, and the power and the glory, for ever and ever.' Amen.

PRAYER 13

The Wings of Prayer

Our Father, thy children who know thee delight themselves in thy presence. We are never happier than when we are near thee. We have found a little heaven in prayer. It has eased our load to tell thee of its weight; it has relieved our wound to tell thee of its smart; it has restored our spirit to confess to thee its wanderings. No place like the mercy seat for us.

We thank thee, Lord, that we have not only found benefit in prayer, but in the answers to it we have been greatly enriched. Thou hast opened thy hid treasures to the voice of prayer; thou hast supplied our necessities as soon as ever we have cried unto thee; yea, we have found it true: 'Before they call I will answer, and while they are yet speaking I will hear'.

We do bless thee, Lord, for instituting the blessed ordinance of prayer. What could we do without it, and we take great shame to ourselves that we should use it so little. We pray that we may be men of prayer, taken up with it, that it may take us up and bear us on its wings towards heaven.

And now at this hour wilt thou hear the voice of our supplication. First, we ask at thy hands, great Father, complete forgiveness for all our trespasses and shortcomings. We hope we can say with truthfulness that we do from our heart forgive all those who have in any way trespassed against us. There lies not in our heart, we hope, a thought of enmity towards any man. However we have been slandered or wronged, we would, with our inmost heart, forgive and forget it all.

We come to thee and pray that, for Jesu's sake, and through the virtue of the blood once shed for many for the remission of sins, thou wouldest give us perfect pardon of every transgression of the past. Blot out, O God, all our sins like a cloud, and let them never be seen again. Grant us also the peace-speaking word of promise applied by the Holy Spirit, that being justified by faith we may have peace with God through Jesus Christ our Lord. Let us be forgiven and know it, and may there remain no lingering question in our heart about our reconciliation with God, but by a firm, full assurance based upon faith in the finished work of Christ, may we stand as forgiven men and women against whom transgression shall be mentioned never again for ever.

And then, Lord, we have another mercy to ask which shall be the burden of our prayer. It is that thou wouldest help us to live such lives as pardoned men should live. We have but a little time to tarry here, for our life is but a vapour - soon it vanishes away; but we are most anxious that we may spend the time of our sojourning here in holy fear, that grace may be upon us from the commencement of our Christian life even to the earthly close of it.

Lord, thou knowest there are some that have not yet begun to live for thee, and the prayer is now offered that they may today be born again. Others have been long in thy ways, and are not weary of them. We sometimes wonder that thou art not weary of us, but assuredly we delight ourselves in the ways of holiness more than ever we did. Oh! that our ways were directed to keep thy statutes without slip or flaw. We wish we were perfectly obedient in thought, and word, and deed, entirely sanctified. We shall never be satisfied till we wake up in Christ's likeness, the likeness of perfection itself. Oh! work us to this self same thing, we beseech thee. May experience teach us more and more how to avoid occasions of sin. May we grow more watchful; may we have a greater supremacy over our own spirit; may we be able to control ourselves under all circumstances, and so act that if the Master were to come at any moment we should not be ashamed to give our account into his hands.

Lord, we are not what we want to be. This is our sorrow. Oh! that thou wouldest, by thy Spirit, help us in the walks of life to adorn the doctrine of God our Saviour in all things. As men of business, as workpeople, as parents, as children, as servants, as masters, whatever we may be, may we be such that Christ may look upon us with pleasure. May his joy be in us, for then only can our joy be full.

Dear Saviour, we are thy disciples, and thou art teaching us the art of living, but we are very dull and very slow, and beside, there is such a bias in our corrupt nature, and there are such examples in the world, and the influence of an ungodly generation tells even upon those that know thee. O dear Saviour, be not impatient with us, but still school us at thy feet, till at last we shall have learned some of the sublime lessons of self-sacrifice, of meekness, humility, fervour, boldness, and love which thy life is fit to teach us. O Lord, we beseech thee mould us into thine own image. Let us live in thee and live like thee. Let us gaze upon thy glory till we are transformed by the sight, and become Christlike among the sons of men.

Lord, hear the confessions of any that have backslidden, who are rather marring thine image than perfecting it. Hear the prayers of any that are conscious of great defects during the past. Give them peace of mind by pardon, but give them strength of mind also to keep clear of such mischief in the future. O Lord, we are sighing and crying more and more after thyself. The more we have of thee, the more we want thee; the more we grow like thee, the more we perceive our defects, and the more we pine after a higher standard, to reach even unto perfection's self.

Oh! help us. Spirit of the living God, continue still to travail in us. Let the groanings that cannot be uttered be still within our spirit, for these are growing pains, and we shall grow while we can sigh and cry, while we can confess and mourn; yet this is not without a blessed hopefulness that he that hath begun a good work in us will perfect it in the day of Christ.

Bless, we pray thee, at this time, the entire church of God in every part of the earth. Prosper the work and service of Christian people, however they endeavour to spread the kingdom of Christ. Convert the heathen, enlighten those that are in any form of error. Bring the entire church back to the original form of Christianity. Make her first pure, and then she shall be united. O Saviour, let thy kingdom come. Oh! that thou wouldest reign, and thy will be done on earth, as it is in heaven.

We pray thee, use every one of us according as we have ability to be used. Take us, and let no talent lie to canker in the treasure house, but may every pound of thine be put out in trading for thee in the blessed market of soul-winning. Oh! give us success. Increase the gifts and graces of those that are saved. Bind us in closer unity to one another than ever. Let peace reign; let holiness adorn us.

Hear us as we pray for all lands, and then for all sorts of men, from the sovereign on the throne to the peasant in the cottage. Let the benediction of heaven descend on men, through Jesus Christ our Lord. Amen.

PRAYER 14

'Bless the Lord, O my soul!'

Lord, we are longing to draw near; may thy Spirit draw us near. We come by the way of Christ our Mediator. We could not approach thee, O our God, if it were not for him, but in him we come boldly to the throne of heavenly grace. Nor can we come without thanksgiving - thanksgiving from the heart, such as the tongue can never express. Thou hast chosen us from before the foundation of the world, and this well-head of mercy sends forth streams of loving-kindness never ceasing. Because we were chosen we have been redeemed with precious blood. Bless the Lord! And we have been called by the Holy Spirit out of the world, and we have been led to obey that wondrous call which hath quickened us and renewed us, and made us the people of God, given us adoption into the divine family. Bless the Lord!

Our hearts would pause as we remember the greatness of each one of thy favours, and we would say, 'Bless the Lord, O my soul, and all that is within me, bless his holy name'. When we consider our utter unworthiness before conversion, and our great faultiness since, we can but admire the riches of abounding grace which God has manifested to us unworthy ones. Bless the Lord! And when we think of all that thou hast promised to give, which our faith embraces as being really ours, since the covenant makes it sure, we know not how abundantly enough to utter the memory of thy great goodness. We would make our praises equal to our expectations, and our expectations equal to thy promises. We can never rise so high. We give to thee, however, the praise of our entire being; unto Jehovah, the God of Abraham, the God of Isaac, and the God of Jacob, the Creator of the world, the Redeemer of men, unto Jehovah be glory forever and ever, and let all his people praise him. Let the redeemed of the Lord say so, whom he hath redeemed from the hand of the enemy.

O Lord, thy works praise thee, but thy saints bless thee; and this shall be our heaven, yea, our heaven of heavens eternally, to praise and magnify the great and ever blessed God. May many a maiden this day, may many a man break forth and say, with the virgin of old, 'My soul doth magnify the Lord and my spirit doth rejoice in God my Saviour'. May there be going up this day sweet incense of praise laid by holy hands, privately upon the altar of God. May the place be filled with the smoke thereof, not perhaps to the consciousness of every one, but to the acceptance of God who shall smell a sweet savour of rest in Christ, and then in the praises of his people in him.

But, Lord, when we have praised thee we have to fold the wing; yea, we have to cover the face and cover the feet and stand before thee to worship in another fashion, for we confess that we are evil, evil in our original, and though renewed by sovereign grace thy people cannot speak of being clean, rid of sin. There is sin which dwelleth in us which is our daily plague. O God, we humble ourselves before thee. We ask that our faith may clearly perceive the blood of the atonement and the covering of the perfect righteousness of Christ; and may we come afresh, depending alone on Jesus. 'I, the chief of sinners am, but Jesus died for me.' May this be our one hope, that Jesus died and rose again, and that for his sake we are accepted in the Beloved.

May every child of thine have his conscience purged from dead works to serve the true and living God. May there be no cloud between us and our heavenly Father; nay, not even a mist, not even the morning mist that soon is gone. May we walk in the light as God is in the light. May our fellowship with the Father and with his Son, Jesus Christ, be unquestionable; may it be fuel; may it fill us with joy; may it be a most real fact this day; may we enjoy it to the full, knowing whom we have believed, knowing who is our Father, knowing who it is that dwells in us, even the Holy Spirit.

Take away from us everything which now might hinder our delighting ourselves in God. May we come to God this day with a supreme joy; may we speak of him as 'God my exceeding joy; yea, mine own God is he'. O God, give us a sense of property in thyself. May we come near to thee, having no doubt and nothing whatsoever that shall spoil the beautiful simplicity of a childlike faith which looks up into the great face of God and saith, 'Our Father, which art in heaven'.

There are those who never repented of sin and never believed in Christ, and consequently the wrath of God abideth on them. They are living without God, they are living in darkness. O God, in thy great mercy look upon them. They do not look at thee, but do thou look at them. May the sinner see his sin and mourn it; see his Saviour and accept him; see himself saved, and go on his way rejoicing. Father, do grant this.

Once more we pray thee, bless thy church. Lord, quicken the spiritual life of believers. Thou hast given to thy church great activity, for which we thank thee. May that activity be supported by a corresponding inner life. Let us not get to be busy here and there with Martha, and forget to sit at thy feet with Mary. Lord, restore to thy church the love of strong doctrine. May thy truth yet prevail. Purge out from among thy church those who would lead others away from the truth as it is in Jesus, and give back the old power and something more. Give us Pentecost, yea, many Pentecosts in one, and may we live to see thy church shine forth clear as the sun and fair as the moon, and terrible as an army with banners.

God, grant that we may live to see better days. But if perilous times should come in these last days make us faithful. Raise up in every country where there has been a faithful church men that will not let the vessel drift upon the rocks. O God of the Judges, thou who didst raise up first one and then another when the people went astray from God; raise up for us still (our Joshuas are dead) our Deborahs, our Baraks, our Gideons and Jephthahs, and Samuels, that shall maintain for God his truth, and worst the enemies of Israel. Lord, look upon thy church in these days. Lord, revive us. Lord, restore us. Lord, give power to thy Word again that thy name may be glorified.

Remember the church of God in this land in all its various phases and portions, and pour out thy Spirit upon it. And wherever thou hast a people may Jesus dwell with them and reveal himself to his own, for Christ's sake, to whom be glory with the Father and with the Holy Ghost, forever and ever. Amen.

PRAYER 15

The Peace of God

Our God, we stand not afar off as Israel did in Sinai, nor does a veil hang dark between thy face and ours, but the veil is rent by the death of our divine Lord and Mediator, Jesus Christ, and in his name we come up to the mercy seat all blood besprinkled, and here we present our prayers and our praises accepted in him. We do confess that we are guilty; we bow our heads and confess that we have broken thy law and the covenant of which it is a part. Didst thou deal with us under the covenant of works none of us could stand. We must confess that we deserve thy wrath and to be banished forever from thy presence. But thou hast made a new covenant, and we come under its divine shadow; we come in the name of Jesus. He is our High Priest; he is our righteousness; he is the well-beloved in whom thou art well pleased.

Holy Spirit, teach us how to pray. Let us know what we should pray for as we ought. Our first prayer is: Be thou adored; reign thou over the whole earth; hallowed be thy name. We desire to see all men submit themselves to thy gracious government. We wish especially that in the hearts of thine own there may be an intense love for thee and a perfect obedience to thee. Grant this to each one of us. We would each one pray, 'Lord, sanctify me; make me obedient; write thy law upon my heart and upon my mind'. Make our nature so clean that temptation cannot defile it. 'Lead us not into temptation, but deliver us from the Evil One.' May our course be very clean, our path be very straight; may we keep our garments unspotted from the world, and in thought and desire and imagination, in will and in purpose, may we be holy as God is holy.

O God, we pray again fulfil that covenant promise, 'I will take away the heart of stone out of your flesh, and I will give you a heart of flesh.' May we be very tender towards thee; may we feel thy faintest monition; may even the gentlest breath of thy Spirit suffice to move us; may we not be 'as the horse or as the mule which have no understanding; whose mouth must be held in with bit and bridle, lest they come near unto us', but may we be as children obedient to a father; may we yield our members cheerfully to be instruments of righteousness; may we have a natural desire wrought in the new nature towards everything that is pure and honest, unselfish and Christly.

O Spirit of God, dwell in us. Is not this also a covenant promise, 'I will put my Spirit within thee, and I will make thee to walk in my ways'. Dwell with us, Holy Spirit; rule over us, Holy Spirit; transform us to thy own likeness, O Holy Spirit! Then shall we be clean; then shall we keep the law. We would offer a prayer to thee for those who are quite strange to the work of the Spirit of God, who have never owned their God, who have lived as if there were no God. Open their eyes that they may see God even though that sight should make them tremble and wish to die. O! let none of us live without our God and Father. Take away the heart of stone, take away the frivolities, the levity, the giddiness of our youth, and give us in downright earnest to seek true happiness where alone it can be found, in reconciliation to God, and in conformity to his will.

Lord, save the careless, save the sinful, the drunkard, take away from him his cups. The unholy and unjust men, deliver these from their filthiness; the dishonest and false, renew them in their lives; and any that are lovers of pleasure, dead while they live, and any that are lovers of self, whose life is bounded by the narrowness of their own being, the Lord renew them, regenerate them, make them new creatures in Christ Jesus. For this we do fervently pray.

Lord God the Holy Ghost, may faith grow in men; may they believe in Christ to the saving of their souls. May their little faith brighten into strong faith, and may their strong faith ripen into the full assurance of faith. May we all have this last blessing; may we believe God fully; may we never waver. Resting in the Great Surety and High Priest of the New Covenant, may we feel 'the peace of God which passeth all understanding', and may we enter into rest.

Bless thy people that are at rest, and deepen that rest. May the rest that thou givest be further enhanced by the rest which they find when they take thy yoke upon them and learn of thee. May thy Word be very sweet to them. May there come over our spirits a deep calm, as when Christ hushed both winds and waves. May we feel not only resignation to thy will, but delight in it, feeling pleased with all the Lord provides. May we rest in our God and be quite happy in the thought that our sins and our iniquities he will remember no more. He has brought us into covenant with him by a covenant which can never fail, so like David we may say this morning: 'Although my house be not so with God, yet he hath made with me an everlasting covenant, ordered in all things and sure'.

Lord, bless thy Word throughout the world. Prosper all missions amongst the heathen, all work among the Mohammedans. And, oh! send thy grace to the churches at home.

Turn the current of thought which sets so strong in the wrong direction, and bring men to love the simplicities of the gospel.

Remember our country in great mercy, and in all ranks and conditions of men do thou give the blessing. May there be multitudes come to Christ from among the poorest of the poor, and let the wealthy be led away from their sin, and brought to Jesus' feet.

'Thy will be done on earth, as it is in heaven; for thine is the kingdom, and the power and the glory, forever and ever.' 'Come, Lord Jesus, come quickly.' All things are in thy hand, come quickly; the cries of thy people persuade thee, 'the Spirit and the bride say, come', make no tarrying, O, our Redeemer, and unto the Father, to the Son, and to the Holy Ghost, the God of Abraham, and God of our Lord Jesus Christ be glory forever and ever. Amen.

PRAYER 16

He ever liveth

Our God, we come to thee by Jesus Christ who has gone within the veil on our behalf and ever liveth to make intercession for us. Our poor prayers could never reach thee were it not for him, but his hands are full of sweet perfume which makes our pleading sweet with thee. His blood is sprinkled on the mercy seat, and now we know that thou dost always hear those who approach thee through that ever blessed name.

We have deeply felt our entire unworthiness even to lift up our eyes to the place where thine honour dwelleth. Thou hast made us to die to our self-righteousness. We pray now because we have been quickened; we have received a new life, and the breath of that life is prayer. We have risen from the dead, and we also make intercession through the life which Christ has given us. We plead with the living God with living hearts because he has made us to live.

Our first prayer shall be for those who do not pray. There is an ancient promise of thine, 'I am found of them that sought me not; I said, Behold me, behold me, to a people that were not a people'. Prove the sovereignty of thy grace, the priority of thy power, which runs before the will of man, by making many willing in this the day of thy power, and calling the things that are not as though they were. May the day come in which they that are in their graves shall hear the voice of God, and they that hear shall live.

How very often thou shewest thy mighty power. O Lord, we bless thee that the voice of God has called many to Christ. Those that were hardened have felt a softness stealing over their spirits; those who were careless have been compelled to sit down and think; those that were wrapped up in earthly things have been compelled to think of eternal things; and thinking, have been disturbed, and driven to despair, but afterwards led to thee, even to thee, dear Saviour, who wast lifted high upon the cross that by thy death sinners might live.

But, Lord, we next would pray that thine own people should know somewhat of the quickening of the Spirit of God. Lord, we thank thee for the very least life to God, for the feeblest ray of faith and glimmering of hope. We are glad to see anything of Christ in any man; but thou hast come, O Saviour, not only that we might have life, but that we might have it more abundantly, so our prayer is that there may be abundance of life.

O make thy people strong in the Lord, in the power of his might. Lord, we find when we walk close with God that we have no desire for the world. When we get away altogether from the things that are seen and temporal, and live upon the invisible and eternal, then we shall have angels' food; nay, better than that, the food of Christ himself, for his flesh is meat indeed, and his blood is drink indeed. Then have we meat to eat that the world knoweth not of. We pray thee raise all our brothers and sisters in Christ into the high and heavenly frame of mind in which they shall be *in* the world and not be *of* it. Whether they have little or much of temporal things, may they be rich in thee and full of joy in the Holy Ghost, and so be blessed men and women.

We pray for some of thine own people who seem to be doing very little for thee. Lord, have mercy upon those whose strength runs towards the world, and who give but little of their strength to the spread of the gospel and the winning of souls. O let none of us fritter away our existence; may we begin to live since Christ hath died; may we reckon that because he died, we died to all the world, and because he lives, we live in newness of life. Lord, we thank thee for that newness of life.

We praise thy name for a new heaven and a new earth; we bless thee that we now see what we never saw before, and hear what we never heard before. Oh! that we might enter into the very secret place of this inner life. May we have as much grace as can be obtained; may we become perfect after the manner of thy servant Paul, but still press forward, seeking still to be more and more conformed to the image of Christ.

Lord, make us useful. Oh! let no believer live to himself. May we be trying to bring others to Christ. May our servants, and work-people, and neighbours all know where we live; and if they do not understand the secret of that life, yet may they see the fruit of that life, and may they ask, 'What is this?' and enquire their way to Christ that they may be sanctified too. O Lord, we pray thee visit thy church. May none of us imagine that we are living aright unless we are bringing others to the cross. Oh! keep us from worldliness; keep us much in prayer; keep us with the light of God shining on our forehead. May we be a happy people, not because screened from affliction, but because we are walking in the light of God.

Again we offer prayer for the many efforts that are scattered abroad today. May they be good wherever they are. We pray for all churches; Lord, revive them all. Wherever Christ is preached, may it be proved that he draws all men unto him. May the preaching of Christ today be peculiarly efficacious. Oh! that thou wouldst raise up many that would preach

Christ, simply, boldly, and with the Holy Ghost sent down from heaven. Send us better days; send us days of refreshing from the presence of the Lord.

Lord, shake the earth with the power of God. Oh! that the heathen lands may hear the Word of God and live. But first convert the church, and then thou wilt convert the world. Oh! deal with those that depart from the faith and grieve thy Holy Spirit. Bring them back again to their first love, and may Christ be fully and faithfully preached everywhere to the glory of his name. Now forgive us every iniquity; now lift us beyond the power of every sin; now lift us to pray and praise; now make the home full of sacred power, and, last of all, come, Lord Jesus. This is the great wish of our souls. Even so, come quickly, come quickly, Lord Jesus. Amen and Amen.

PRAYER 17

To be like Christ

Blessed art thou, O God; teach us thy statutes! Because thou art the infinitely blessed One, thou canst impart blessing, and thou art infinitely willing to do so, and therefore do we approach thee with great confidence, through Jesus Christ thy Son, whom thou hast made blessed for evermore.

Oh! hear thou the voice of thy servants this day, and according to thine infinite love and wisdom answer thou us; according to thy riches in glory, by Christ Jesus.

First we would confess before thee, O God, the sin we have committed, mourning over it. Touch each one's heart now with tenderness that every one of us may lament that thou shouldst even have a few things against us, if they be but few, for in the great love of our blessed Master he said to his churches, 'Nevertheless, I have a few things against thee'. O Lord, if thou hast so kept us by thy grace that there have been but a few things against us, yet help us to bewail them much. O infinite Love, can we sin against thee at all? How debased is our nature then! Forgive, sweet Saviour, more fully, that we may live thy life while we are here among the sons of men, for as thou art, even so also are we in this world, and we wish the parallel to become more close and perfect every day!

Forgive those who have never felt the guilt of sin, who are living in it, who are carnally minded, who are therefore dead.

O, quicken by thy divine Spirit; take away the pleasure which they feel in sin; deliver them from being the bond slaves of it. Alas! we know the sorrow of sometimes being captured by it, but still we are not yet slaves. The Spirit, the life of God, in Jesus Christ, hath made us free from the law of sin and death. O, deliver others; bring them up out of the horrible pit of sin. Deliver them from the death of their natures and save them by the Spirit of the living God, and apply the precious blood of Jesus to their hearts and consciences.

And, Lord, hear us who are thy children, in whom the Spirit beareth witness with our spirit, that we are the children of God. Hear us while we bring before thee our daily struggles. Blessed be thy name; there are some sins which thou hast helped us to overcome, and now they are trodden beneath our feet with many a tear that we ever should have been in bondage to them. And O! there are rebellions within our nature still. We think that we are getting holy, and behold we discover that we are under the power of pride, that we are self-conceited about ourselves. Lord, help us to master pride.

And then when we try to be humble before thee we find ourselves falling into inaction and supineness. Lord, slay sloth within us, and never let us find a pillow in the doctrines of grace for ease while yet a single sin remains. Besides, great God, the raging lusts of the flesh will sometimes pounce upon us like wild beasts. Help us to be very watchful lest by any means we be torn and rent by them. O keep us, we beseech thee, Lord, for without thy keeping we cannot keep ourselves.

Alas! we are even sometimes subject to unbelief. If trials come which we expected not, or if the body grows faint, how liable we are to begin to doubt the faithful promise, and so to grieve the Holy Spirit. Lord, we cannot bear this; we cannot bear this; it is not enough for us that our garments are clean, and that we walk uprightly before men; we long to walk before thee in such a way that there will be nothing to grieve thy Spirit, nothing to vex the tender love of our Beloved. O, come, divine Spirit, and exercise thy cleansing power upon it according to thy promise, 'I will cleanse thy blood which I have not cleansed, saith the Lord, that dwelleth in Zion'.

O that everything might help us towards purity, for we crave after it; we mind the things of the Spirit, and there is groaning within us to be utterly delivered from the things of the flesh, that we may in spirit, soul and body, be a cleansed temple fit for the indwelling of the Holy One of Israel. Lord, help us, we pray thee, in our daily life to be as Christ was. If we are men of sorrows, may there be that lustre about our sorrow which there was about his in patience and holy submission to the divine law. If we are men of activity, may our activity be like his, for he 'went about doing good'. May we seek in all ways the good of our fellow men and the glory of our God.

We wish that the zeal of thine house would eat us up; that we should be full of sacred warmth; that our lips were touched with the live coal so that there be fire in us perpetually flaming and burning, and ourselves a living sacrifice unto God.

Bless us, we pray thee, as to our example and influence. May it always be of a salutary kind; may there be sweetness and light about us which all must be obliged to perceive. Not for our honour would we crave this, but that our light may so shine before men that they may 'see our good works and glorify our Father which is in heaven'. The Lord grant us this!

We beseech thee, bless the unconverted among us; bring them in, dear Saviour, bring them in. Help the living among us to compel them to come in that thy house may be filled; may something of a sacred compulsion be used that they may not be left outside to starve in the highways and hedges, but be brought in to the gospel feast.

The Lord bless our country at this time. Wilt thou be gracious unto those who have the helm of affairs that in the midst of great difficulty they may be wisely and graciously directed. Bless other countries, too, for whom we do most earnestly pray. The Lord bless the whole church of Christ, and especially all missionaries that are labouring in the foreign field.

O, Saviour, let thy kingdom come. When will this earth be delivered from the incubus of superstition and of infidelity? O that thou wouldst hear creation's groans and come quickly. O thou great Deliverer, joy of the earth art thou, the expected of the tribes of the Israel still; come, we beseech thee, thou absent love, thou dear unknown, thou fairest of ten thousand fair; come a second time to earth and to the sons of men, and especially to thy Bride, the church. Even so come quickly, Lord Jesus. Amen.

PRAYER 18

O, for more grace!

Our Father, thou dost hear us when we pray. Thou hast provided an advocate and intercessor in heaven now; we cannot come to thee unless thy Holy Spirit shall suggest desire, and help us while we plead. We would ask that the subject which caused such conflict to Paul may be beyond conflict with us; may we know the Christ and have him to be our all in all. We would have the conflict about others, but may we be past it for ourselves. He is everything to us; more than all in him we find.

We do accept thee, Lord Jesus, to be made unto us wisdom, righteousness, sanctification and redemption. We will not look out of thee for anything, for everything is in thee. Our sin is pardoned; our sinful nature is subdued; we have a perfect righteousness; we have an immortal life; we have a sure hope; we have an immovable foundation. Why should we look beyond thee? Why should we look within to ourselves, knowing that thou shalt be the only well from which we will draw the living water, the only foundation upon which we will be builded. We would thrust out new rootlets this day, and take fresh hold on the blessed soil in which grace has planted us.

O Saviour, reveal thyself anew, teach us a little more, help us to go a little deeper into the divine mystery. May we grip thee and grasp thee; may we suck out of thee the nutriment of our spirit; may we be in thee as a branch is in the stem, and may we bear fruit from thee. Without thee we can do nothing.

Forgive, we pray thee, thy servants, any wanderings during the past. If we have forgotten thee, forget us not; if we have acted apart from thee, forgive the act. Blot out the sin. Help us in the future to live only as we live in thee, to speak, and even to think, as in union with our living Head. Take away from us all life which is contrary to the life of Christ; bring us into complete subjection in him, until for us to live shall be Christ in every single act of life. May we walk humbly with God in joyful faith in the finished work of Christ.

Saviour, look on thy beloved ones, and give blessings according to our necessities. We cannot pray a prayer that would comprise all, but thou canst, great Intercessor, plead for each one, and get for each one of us the blessing wanted. Are we depressed? Give us stronger faith. Have we become worldly? Pardon this great offence and lead us more into spiritual things. Have we become joyous, but have forgotten the source of joy? Lord, sweeten and savour that joy with the sweet perfume of thine own presence. Have we to preach, and do we feel weak? Oh! be our strength. Are we engaged in the Sunday-school, and have we seen little success? Lord, teach us how to teach; give us our boys and girls to be our spiritual reward. Are we sickly? Have we those that vex us because they are unholy and ungodly? This, indeed, is a terrible trial to many; Lord, help them, both in their personal sickness and in this great spiritual trouble. Have we dear ones whom we love with all our hearts, who pine before our eyes? Lord, have pity upon them and restore them, and give them patience to bear pain; and give us resignation to thy will in this matter. Whatever the trial of thy servants, make a way of escape that we may be able to bear it.

Our great concern, however, is to grow in grace and to become like our Master. We struggle and we struggle, but how small our progress! Lord, help us in any matter in which we have felt defeated. If we have been betrayed through want of watchfulness, Lord, forgive and help another time. If any of thy servants have lost the brightness of their evidence, give them to come to Christ as sinners if they cannot come as saints. And if through Satan's temptation any are sorely put to it even to keep their feet, hold them up; and if any have fallen, help them to say, 'Rejoice not against me, O mine enemy; when I fall I shall arise'.

Now look in great mercy upon those who are unconverted; Lord, save them. Some are quite careless; Lord, they are dead; come and quicken them. We cannot see, but thou canst. Oh! that some of the most obdurate and hardened might be softened by the touch of thy Spirit this very day; and may others who are not careless, but who are even seeking after eternal life, but who are going the wrong way to work, may they be shown their error, may they be led in the way by thee, may they look, and, looking, live. We know how many of them are wanting to be this and that before they take Christ to be all in all; may they cease their seeking by finding everything in Christ. As thou art a prayer-hearing God, and a God of pardon, issue many a pardon from thy heavenly court today, sealed with the Redeemer's blood, signed with the Father's name. Oh! today, Lord, ere men grow old in sin, ere they die in their sins, save them with an everlasting salvation.

God bless our country. God bless this city; may there be no disquietude between the different orders of men - the employer and the employed; but may there be a general spirit of goodwill given to the people of this city, and do thou prosper us.

Remember all people, especially the poor, the widows and the fatherless, and any that are depressed in spirit, whose depression tends to the failure of reason; the Lord restore them, and such as are dying. O Lord, let them not die without hope, and may thy believing people learn to pass away without even tasting the bitterness of death. May they enter into rest, each one walking in his own uprightness.

Save this age from its own intellectual pride; give back the spirit of simple faith in Christ, for we desire his glory. 'For thine is the kingdom, and the power, and the glory, forever and ever. Amen.'

PRAYER 19

God's unspeakable gift

O Lord, many of us feel like the lame man at the Beautiful Gate of the temple. Come by this way and make the lame ones perfectly sound. O Lord, thou canst do by thy servants today what thou didst by them in the olden time. Work miracles of mercy even upon outer court worshippers who are too lame to get into the holy place.

But there are many who feel like that man when he was restored. We would follow our Restorer, the Prince of Life, into the temple, leaping and walking and praising God. He has gone into the temple in the highest sense, up to the throne of God. He climbs, and we would follow, up the steps of the temple one by one, made meet. We would come nearer and nearer to the throne of God.

O Lord, thou hast done such great things for us that we feel the drawings of thy love. 'The Lord hath appeared of old unto me, saying: Yea, I have loved thee with an everlasting love, therefore with loving-kindness have I drawn thee.'

Draw us nearer, Lord, draw us into the inner sanctuary; draw us within the place which once was hidden by the veil which Christ has rent; bring us right up to the throne of grace, and there beholding the glory of God above the Mercy Seat may we have communion with the Most High. Heal all our diseases and forgive us all our trespasses.

Still, Lord, though healed of a former lameness so that now we have strength, we need a further touch from thee; we are so apt to get dull and stupid; come and help us, Lord Jesus. A vision of thy face will brighten us, but to feel thy Spirit touching us will make us vigorous. Oh! for the leaping and the walking of the man born lame. May we today dance with holy joy like David before the Ark of God. May a holy exhilaration take possession of every part of us; may we be glad in the Lord; may our mouth be filled with laughter, and our tongue with singing, 'for the Lord hath done great things for us whereof we are glad'.

Today help thy people to put on Christ. May we live as those who are alive from the dead, for he is the quickening Spirit; and may we feel him to be so. Is any part of us still dead, Lord, quicken it. May the life which has taken possession of our heart take possession of our head; may the brain be active in holy thought; may our entire being, indeed, respond to the life of Christ, and may we live in newness of life.

We would fain fall down on our faces and worship the Son of God today. It is such a wonder that he should have loved us; and he has done such wonderful things for us and in us that we may still call him God's unspeakable gift. He is unspeakably precious to our souls. Thou knowest all things, Lord; thou knowest that we love thee. May that love bubble up today like a boiling cauldron, may our hearts overflow; and if we cannot speak what we feel, may that holy silence be eloquent with the praise of God.

Lord, send thy life throughout the entire church. Lord, visit thy church, restore sound doctrine, restore holy and earnest living. Take away from professors their apparent love for frivolities, their attempts to meet the world on its own ground, and give back the old love to the doctrines of the cross, the doctrines of the Christ of God; and once more may free grace and dying love be the music that shall refresh the church, and make her heart exceeding glad.

Just now when the earth is waking up to life, Lord, wake up dead hearts, and if there are seeds of grace lying dormant in any soul may they begin to bud, may the bulb down at the heart send forth its golden cup and drink in of the light, the life of God. Oh! save today. 'Thy King in the midst of thee is mighty: he will save'. Our very heart is speaking now much more loudly and sweetly than our lips can speak. Lord, save sinners; great High Priest, have compassion on the ignorant and such as are out of the way. Great Shepherd of the sheep, gather the lambs within thine arm; find out the lost sheep; throw them on thy shoulders and bring them home rejoicing.

We pray also for the poorest and the down-trodden. The Lord look upon the poor of this world, and make them rich in faith, and comfort them in heart by the Holy Ghost. Let thy light and thy truth go forth to the most distant parts of the earth; 'let the people praise thee; O God, let all the people praise thee'. Give us the times of refreshing. May we have a visit from Christ by the power of his Spirit; and until he come may there be a blessed halcyon time of peace and salvation.

'Thy kingdom come, thy will be done, on earth, as it is in heaven.' And do thou come thyself, great King. May our eyes, if it please thee, behold thee on earth; but if not, if we fall asleep ere that blessed array, we can say, 'I know that my Redeemer liveth; and though after my skin worms destroy this body, yet in my flesh shall I see God.'

Bless every Sunday-school teacher, every tract distributor, every open-air preacher. Bless, we pray thee, all Bible-women and nurses, deacons and missionaries of the City Mission, Bible readers and all others who in any way seek to bring men to Christ. O God the Holy Ghost, work mightily, we pray thee; flood the world with a baptism of thy power, and 'let the whole earth be filled with a knowledge of the Lord as the waters cover the sea'. We ask all in that dear name which made the lame man whole, which is sweet to God in heaven and dear to us below; and unto Father, Son and Holy Ghost be glory, world without end. Amen.

PRAYER 20

The Great Sacrifice

O God our Father, we do remember well when we were called to thee; with many sweet and wooing voices we were bidden to return. Thou didst thyself hang out the lights of mercy that we might know the way home, and thy dear Son himself came down to seek us. But we wandered still. It brings the tears to our eyes to think that we should have been so foolish and so wicked, for we often extinguished the light within and conscience we tried to harden, and we sinned against light and knowledge with a high hand against our God.

Thou hast often brought us very low even to our knees, and we cried for mercy, but we rose to sin again. Blessed was that day when thou didst strike the blow of grace - the effectual blow. Then didst thou wither up our comeliness and all our perfection was rolled in the dust. We saw ourselves to be slain by the law, to be lost, ruined and undone, and then we rolled to and fro in the tempests of our thoughts and staggered like drunken men, and were at our wits' end - then did we cry unto thee in our trouble, and blessed be thy name forever, thou didst deliver us.

O happy day that sealed our pardon with the precious blood of Jesus, accepted by faith. We would recall the memory of that blessed season by repeating it. We come again now to the cross whereon the Saviour bled; we give another look of faith to him. We trust we never take away our eyes off him, but if we have done so we would look anew; we would gaze onto the body of the Son of God, pierced with nails, parched with thirst, bleeding, dying, because 'it pleased the Father to bruise him; he hath put him to grief'.

Lord God, we see in thy crucified Son a sacrifice for sin; we see how thou hast made him to be sin for us that we might be made the righteousness of God in him, and we do over again accept him to be everything to us. This is the victim by whose blood the covenant is made through faith; this is that paschal Lamb by the sprinkling of whose blood all Israel is secured; for thou hast said, 'When I see the blood I will pass over you'. This is the blood which gives us access into that which is within the veil; this is the blood which now to our souls is drink indeed, and we do rejoice in the joy which this new wine of the covenant hath given unto our spirits.

We would take afresh the cup of salvation and call upon the name of the Lord. We would pay our vows now in the midst of all the Lord's people and in the courts of his house; and this is a part payment of our vow that we bless the Lord Jesus who hath put away our sin. We bless him that he hath redeemed us unto himself not with corruptible things as silver and gold, but with his own precious blood; and we do avow ourselves today to be the Lord's.

We are not our own; we are bought with a price. Lord Jesus, renew thy grasp of us, take us over again, for we do even with greater alacrity than ever before surrender ourselves to thee, and so 'bind the sacrifice with cords, even with cords to the horns of the altar'. O Lord, I am thy servant, and the son of thine handmaid. Thou hast loosed my bonds. The Lord liveth, and blessed be my Rock. Henceforth within that Rock I hide myself. For him I live. The Lord enable all his people with sincere hearts, with undivided hearts, thus again to give themselves up to Jesus, and do thou set in them anew the marks and tokens of thy possession till every one of us shall say as many of us can say, 'From henceforth let no man trouble me; for I bear in my body the marks of the Lord Jesus Christ'.

We bless thee, Lord, for that mark to which some of us can look back with much joy. It is not in our hand, nor in our forehead, nor on our foot, nor on our heart alone; our whole body has been buried with Christ in baptism unto death, and now the whole body, soul and spirit, by our willing consecration, belong unto Christ henceforth and forever.

Our Father, there is one prayer which has kept rising to our lip even while we have been thus speaking to thee. It comes from our very heart. It is: Bring others to thyself. Hast thou not said, O God of Jacob, 'Yet will I gather others unto him that have not been gathered'? Hast thou not given to thy Son the heathen for his inheritance, and the uttermost parts of the earth for his possession? Lord, give thy Son the reward of his travail; give him a part of that reward this day wherever he is preached. Oh! that some might be moved with the love of Christ.

Lord, some know not who thou art; convince them of thy deity and thy power to save. Lord, many of them do not think; they live as if they were to die, and there would be an end of them. O divine Spirit, convince them of judgment to come. Set before each careless eye that day of terrible pomp when for every idle word that men shall speak they must give an account. O divine Spirit, teach unreasonable men true reason; teach the obdurate sensitiveness; look upon them, Jesus, just as thou didst on those of the synagogue, not with anger, but still being grieved because of the hardness of their hearts. 'Father, forgive them, they know not what they do', and bring many, many, many this very day to the dear feet that were nailed to the cross. Oh! how we long for it. Deny us what thou wilt, only bring sinners to thyself.

Lord Jesus, thou art gone from us. We rejoice that this is the fact, for thou hast taught us that it is expedient for us that thou shouldest go, and that the Comforter should be with us; but, oh! let us not miss that promised presence of the Comforter. May he be here to help and succour in all works of faith and labours of love, and may we feel that he has come among us and is dwelling with us because he is convincing the world of sin, of righteousness and of judgment to come.

O Spirit of God, bring men to accept the great propitiation, to see their sin washed away in the purple flood whose fount was opened when the heart of Christ was pierced, and may blood-washed sinners begin to sing on earth that everlasting anthem which shall be sung by all the redeemed in heaven.

We beseech thee now, Lord, to look upon all thy people and grant every one a blessing. Some are in great trouble. Deliver them, we pray thee. Others may be in great peril, though they have no trouble. The Lord save his people from the evils of prosperity. It may be some of thine own people find it hard to worship because of cares; may they be able, like Abraham, when the birds came down upon the sacrifice, to drive them away.

O Spirit of God, make us all more holy. Work in us more completely the image of Christ. We do long to be as the Lord Jesus Christ in spirit and temper, and in unselfishness of life. Give us the character of Christ, we pray thee. Redemption from the power of sin is purchased with his blood, and we crave for it, and pray that we may daily receive it. Let the whole militant church of Christ be blessed; put power into all faithful ministries; convert this country; save it from abounding sin; let all the nations of the earth know the Lord, but especially bless those nations that speak our own dear mother tongue, where our same Lord and Christ is worshipped this day after the same fashion.

The Lord bless his people. Bring the church to break down all bonds of nationality, all limits of sects, and may we feel the blessed unity which is the very glory of the church of Christ; yea, let the whole earth be filled with his glory. Our prayer can never cease until we reach this point: 'thy Kingdom come, thy will be done, on earth as it is in heaven'. Nothing less than this can we ask for. And now hear us as we pray for the sovereign and all in authority, and ask thy blessing to rest upon this land, and let thy blessing extend over all the family of man. We ask it for Christ's sake. Amen.

PRAYER 21

Boldness at the throne of grace

O God! we would not speak to thee as from a distance, nor stand like trembling Israel under the law at a distance from the burning mount, for we have not come unto Mount Sinai, but unto Mount Sion, and that is a place for holy joy and thankfulness, and not for terror and bondage. Blessed be thy name, O Lord! We have learnt to call thee 'Our Father, which art in heaven'; so there is reverence, for thou art in heaven; but there is sweet familiarity, for thou art our Father.

We would draw very near to thee now through Jesus Christ the Mediator, and we would make bold to speak to thee as a man speaketh with his friend, for hast thou not said by thy Spirit, 'Let us come boldly unto the throne of the heavenly grace'. We might well start away and flee from thy face if we only remembered our sinfulness. Lord! we do remember it with shame and sorrow; we are grieved to think we should have offended thee, should have neglected so long thy sweet love and tender mercy; but we have now returned unto the 'shepherd and bishop of our souls'. Led by such grace, we look to him whom we crucified, and we have mourned for him and then have mourned for our sin.

Now, Lord, we confess our guilt before thee with tenderness of heart, and we pray thee seal home to every believer here that full and free, that perfect and irreversible charter of forgiveness which thou gavest to all them that put their trust in Jesus Christ. Lord! thou hast said it: 'If we confess our sins, he is faithful and just to forgive us our sins, and to save us from all unrighteousness'. There is the sin confessed: there is the ransom accepted: we therefore know we have peace with God, and we bless that glorious one who hath come 'to finish transgression, to make an end of sin', to bring in everlasting righteousness, which righteousness by faith we take unto ourselves and thou dost impute unto us.

Now, Lord, wilt thou be pleased to cause all thy children's hearts to dance within them for joy? Oh! help thy people to come to Jesus again today. May we be looking unto him today as we did at the first. May we never take off our eyes from his divine person, from his infinite merit, from his finished work, from his living power, or from the expectancy of his speedy coming to 'judge the world in righteousness and the people with his truth'.

Bless all thy people with some special gift, and if we might make a choice of one it would be this: 'Quicken us, O Lord, according to thy Word'. We have life; give it to us more abundantly. Oh, that we might have so much life that out of the midst of us there might flow rivers of living water. The Lord make us useful. Do, dear Saviour, use the very least among us; take the one talent and let it be put out to interest for the great Father. May it please thee to show each one of us what thou wouldest have us to do. In our families, in our business, in the walks of ordinary life may we be serving the Lord, and may we often speak a word for his name, and help in some way to scatter the light amongst the ever-growing darkness; and ere we go hence may we have sown some seed which we shall bring with us on our shoulders in the form of sheaves of blessing.

O God! bless our Sunday-schools, and give a greater interest in such work, that there may be no lack of men and women who shall be glad and happy in the work of teaching the young. Do impress this, we pray thee, upon thy people just now. Move men who have gifts and ability also to preach the gospel. There are many that live in villages, and there is no gospel preaching near them. Lord! set them preaching themselves. Wilt thou move some hearts so powerfully that their tongues cannot be quiet any longer, and may they attempt in some way, either personally or by supporting some one, to bring the gospel into dark benighted hamlets that the people may know the truth.

O Lord! stir up the dwellers in this great, great city. Oh! arouse us to the spiritual destitution of the masses. O God, help us all by some means, by any means, by every means to get at the ears of men for Christ's sake that so we may reach their hearts. We would send up an exceeding great and bitter cry to thee on behalf of the millions that enter no place of worship, but rather violate its sanctity and despise its blessed message. Lord! wake up London, we beseech thee. Send us another Jonah; send us another John the Baptist. Oh! that the Christ himself would send forth multitudes of labourers amongst this thick standing corn, for the harvest truly is plenteous, but the labourers are few. O God! save this city; save this country; save all countries; and let thy kingdom come; may every knee bow and confess that Jesus Christ is Lord.

Our most earnest prayers go up to heaven to thee now for great sinners, for men and women that are polluted and depraved by the filthiest of sins. With sovereign mercy make a raid amongst them. Come and capture some of these that they may become great lovers of him that shall forgive them, and may they become great champions for the cross.

Lord, look upon the multitudes of rich people in this city that know nothing about the gospel and do not wish to know. Oh! that somehow the poor rich might be rich with the gospel of Jesus Christ. And then, Lord, look upon the multitude of the poor and the working classes that think religion to be a perfectly unnecessary thing for them. Do, by some means we pray thee, get them to think and bring them to listen that faith may come by hearing, and hearing by the Word of God.

Above all, O Holy Spirit, descend more mightily. Would, God, thou wouldest flood the land till there should be streams of righteousness; for is there not a promise, 'I will pour water upon him that is thirsty and floods upon the dry ground'. Lord, set thy people praying; stir up the church to greater prayerfulness.

Now, as thou hast bidden us, we pray for the people among whom we dwell. We pray for those in authority, for thy benediction to all judges and rulers as also upon the poorest of the poor and the lowest of the low. Lord, bless the people; let the people praise thee, O God! Yea, let all the people praise thee, for Jesus Christ's sake. Amen and Amen.

PRAYER 22

The presence of God

Our Father, which art in heaven, our hearts are full of gratitude to thee for thy Word. We bless thee that we have it in our houses, that thou hast given to many of us to understand it and to enjoy it. Although as yet we know not what we shall know, yet have we learned from it what we can never forget, that which has changed our lives, has removed our burdens, has comforted our hearts, has set our faces like flints against sin and made us eager after perfect holiness.

We thank thee, Lord, for every leaf of the book, not only for its promises which are inexpressibly sweet, but for its precepts in which our soul delights, and especially for the revelation of thy Son, our Lord and Saviour Jesus Christ. O God, we thank thee for the manifestation of him even in the types and shadows of the Old Testament. These are inexpressibly glorious to us, full of wondrous value, inexpressibly dear because in them and through them we see the Lord. But we bless thee much more for the clear light of the New Testament, for giving us the key to all the secrets of the Old Testament, for now, reading the Scriptures of the new covenant, we understand the language of the old covenant and are made to joy and to rejoice therein.

Father, we thank thee for the Book, we thank thee for the glorious Man, the God whom the Book reveals as our Saviour;

and now we thank thee for the blessed Spirit for without his light upon the understanding we should have learned nothing. The letter killeth, it is the Spirit that giveth life. Blessed are our eyes that have been touched with heavenly eye-salve. Blessed are the hearts that have been softened, that have been made ready to receive the truth in the love of it! Blessed be the sovereign grace of God that hath chosen unto him a people who delight in his Word and who meditate in it both day and night!

Our hearts are full of praise to God for this Man of truth, for this unmeasured wealth of holy knowledge. Lord, make us to enjoy it more and more. May we feed upon this manna; may we drink from this well of life; may we be satisfied with it, and by it be made like to the God from whom it came.

And now, Lord, our prayer is to thee at the mention of thy sacred Book, that thou wouldst write it upon the fleshly tablets of our heart more fully. We want to know the truth that the truth may make us free. We want to feel the truth that we may be sanctified by it. Oh! let it be in us a living seed which shall produce in us a life acceptable before God, a life which shall be seen in everything that we do unto the living God, for we remember that thou art not the God of the dead but of the living.

Lord, we ask that thy Word may chasten us whenever we go astray, may it enlighten us whenever for a moment we get into darkness. May thy Word be the supreme ruler of our being. May we give ourselves up to its sacred law to be obedient to its every hint, wishing in all things, even in the least things, to do the will of God from the heart and having every thought brought into captivity to the mind of the Spirit of God.

Bless thy people; bless them in this way by saturating them

with the Word of thy truth. O Lord, they are out in the world so much. Oh! grant that the world may not take them off from their God. May they get the world under their feet; let them not be buried in it, but may they live upon it, treading it beneath their feet, the spiritual getting the mastery always over the material. Oh! that the Word of God might be with us when we are in the midst of an ungodly generation. May the Proverbs often furnish us with wisdom, the Psalms furnish us with comfort, the Gospels teach us the way of holiness, and the Epistles instruct us in the deep things of the kingdom of God.

Lord, educate us for a higher life, and let that life be begun here. May we be always in the school, always disciples, and when we are out in the world may we be trying to put in practice what we have learned at Jesu's feet. What he tells us in darkness may we proclaim in the light, and what he whispers in our ear in the closets may we sound forth upon the house-tops.

Oh! dear, dear Saviour, what could we do without thee? We are as yet in banishment, we have not come into the land of light and glory; it is on the other side of the river, in the land where thou dwellest, thy land of Immanuel, and till we come thither be thou with us. We have said unto ourselves, How shall we live without our Lord; and then we have said unto thee, 'If thy Spirit go not with us, carry us not up hence'. Oh! be to us this day as the fiery cloudy pillar that covered all the camp of Israel. May we dwell in God; may we live and move in God; may we be conscious of the presence of God to a greater extent than we are conscious of anything else.

Bless the churches. Look on them, Lord; cast an eye of love upon the little companies of the faithful wherever they may be and help them and their pastors, and may the churches be in every place a light in the midst of this crooked and perverse generation. O God, we are waiting and watching for a display of thy great power among the people.

It is an age of great luxury and great sin and gross departures from the truth; we beseech thee defend thine own. When thine ark was carried captive among the Philistines and set up in the temple of Dagon, Dagon fell before it; then didst thou smite thine adversaries in the hinder parts and put them to a perpetual reproach, and thou canst do the like again, and we pray it may be so. Oh! for the stretched out hand of God. We are longing to see it in the conversion of great multitudes by the gospel, that those who have said, 'Aha, aha, the gospel has lost its power' may be made foolish by the wisdom of the Most High, even as Jannes and Jambres were made foolish when they could not do so with their enchantments, but God was with his servant.

O Jehovah, thou art the true God, God of Abraham, and of Isaac, and of Jacob, this God is our God forever and ever; he shall be our guide even unto death. Thou who spakest by the apostles speak still by thy servants, and let thy Word be with as much power as when thou saidst, 'Let there be light, and there was light'. Oh! for the lifting up of thy voice! Let confusion and darkness once again hear the voice of him that makes order and that giveth life. Oh! how we would stir thee up, thou gracious God. Our prayers would take the form of that ancient one, 'Awake, awake, put on thy strength'. Art thou not he that cut Egypt and wounded the crocodile? Hast thou not still the same power to smite and to vindicate thine own truth and deliver thine own redeemed?

O Lamb, slain from before the foundation of the world, thou art still to sit upon the throne, for he that is on the throne looks like a Lamb that has been newly slain. O Jesus, we beseech thee, take to thyself thy great power; divide the spoil with the strong; take the purchase of thy precious blood and rule from the river even unto the ends of the earth.

Here we are before thee; look on us in great pity. Lord, bless thine own people. With favour do thou compass them as with a shield. Lord, save the unsaved. In great compassion draw them by the attractive magnet of the cross, draw them to thyself, compel them to come in that the wedding may be furnished with guests.

With one heart we put up our prayer on the behalf of the teachers of the young. We thank thee, Lord, that so many men and women are ready to give their Sabbath's rest to this important service. Oh! grant that zeal for teaching the young may never burn low in the church. May any that are taking no part in it and who ought to be, be aroused at once to commence the holy effort. Bless the teachers of the senior classes; may their young men and women pass into the church; may there be no gap between the school and the church. Bridge that distance by thy sovereign grace. But equally bless the teachers of the infants and of the younger children. May conversion go on among the young. May there be multitudes of such conversions. In effect, we would pray that no child may leave the schools unsaved. Oh! save the children, great Lover of the little ones. Thou who wouldst have them suffered to come unto thee, thou wilt not forget them, but thou wilt draw them and accept them. Lord, save the children! Let all the schools participate in the blessing which we seek, and by this blessed agency may this nation be kept from heathenism; this city especially be preserved from its dogged disregard of the Sabbath, and its carelessness about the things of God. Oh! bless the Sabbath-school to London, to every part of it, and let Jesus Christ be glorified among the little ones, and again may there be heard loud hosannas in the streets of Jerusalem from the babes and sucklings out of whose mouths thou hast ordained strength. The Lord be with these dear workers throughout today and make it a high day, a festival of prayer and faith, a time when Jesus the Lord shall especially meet with them and bless them.

God bless our country! Grant guidance at this time to all with regard to the political affairs of this nation. Grant thy blessing to all ranks and conditions of men, and let every nation call thee 'blessed'. Let all tongues speak the name of Jesus and all men own him as Lord and King. We ask it in his name. Amen.

PRAYER 23

The Look of Faith

Our Father, we have listened to thy gracious words. Truly thy paths drop fatness. Wherever thou art, mercy abounds. Before thy feet rivers of grace spring up. When thou comest to man it is with the fullness of pardoning love. Thou hast bidden us come to thee and seek thee while thou mayest be found. We would come now. May thy Holy Spirit help us! May Jesus lead the way and be our Mediator now!

Blessed be thy name; there are many who sought thy face many years ago. We have since then tasted that thou art gracious, and we know by a delightful experience that thou dost indeed give milk and honey to such as trust thee. Oh! we wish we had known thee earlier.

Lord, thou hast been full of truth and faithfulness to us throughout every step of our journey, and though thou hast not withheld the rod of the covenant from us, we are as grateful for that this morning as for the kisses of thy lips. Thou hast dealt well with thy servants according to thy Word. Blessed be thy name forever and ever.

But there are some who have never come to thee; they are hearers, but hearers only; they have listened to gracious invitations thousands of times, but they have never accepted them. Say unto them, 'Thereto hast thou gone, but no further shalt thou proceed in thy carelessness and trifling. Here shalt thou stay and turn unto thy God'. O Saviour, thou hast all power in heaven and earth, therefore thou canst through the preaching of thy Word influence the hearts of men. Turn them, and they shall be turned. Oh! do it this day.

We would now in our prayers come; as we came at first would we come again; we would renew our vows, we would again repeat our repentance and our faith, and then look at the brazen serpent and touch but the border of thy garment. We would begin again. O Lord, help us to do it in sincerity and truth. And first we do confess that we are by nature lost and by practice ruined. We are altogether as an unclean thing, and all our righteousnesses are as filthy rags. We would lie at those dear pierced feet bleeding at heart because of sin, wounded, mangled, crushed by the fall and by our own transgression. We confess that if thou shouldst number our sins upon us and deal with us accordingly we should be sent to the lowest hell.

We have no merit, no claim, no righteousness of our own. Oh! now, dear Saviour, we look up to thee. Oh! that some might look for the first time, and those of us that have long looked would fix our happy gaze again upon that blessed substitutionary sacrifice wherein is all our hope. Dear Saviour, we do take thee to be everything to us, our sin-bearer and our sin-destroyer. We have not a shadow of a shade of a hope anywhere but in thyself, thy life, thy death, thy resurrection, thine ascension, thy glory, thy reign, thy second advent; these are the only stars in our sky.

We look up to thee and are filled with light. But O thou dear, dear Saviour, we dare not turn to ordinances, we dare not turn to our own prayers, and tears, and almsgivings, we dare not look to our own works, we only look to thee; thy wounds, Immanuel, these bleed the balm that heals our wounds, thy crowned head once girt with thorns, thy body once laid in the silent tomb, thy Godhead once covered and concealed from man, but now resplendent amidst triumphant hosts. If we can perish trusting in thee we must perish, but we know we cannot, for thou hast bound up our salvation with thy glory, and because thou art a glorious Saviour forever, none that trust in thee shall ever be confounded.

But we do trust thee now. If all our past experience has been a mistake, yet we will begin at the cross today; or if we have never had any experience of thee before we would begin today. Oh! hear thou, hear thou the prayer:

> Dear Saviour, draw reluctant hearts,
> To thee let sinners fly.

By his agony and bloody sweat, by his cross and passion, by his precious death and burial, we beseech thee hear us now! We plead with thee for some that are not pleading for themselves. O Spirit of God, let it not be so any longer. Now sweetly use thy key to open the fast-closed door, and come into men's hearts and dwell there that they may live. We have a thousand things to ask. We should like to plead for our country and for all countries; we should like to plead with thee for the sick and for the dying, for the poor and for the fatherless. We have innumerable blessings to ask, but somehow they all go away from our prayer just now, and this is our one cry: Save, Lord, we beseech thee, even now send salvation! Come Holy Spirit to open blind eyes and unstop deaf ears and quicken dead hearts.

Father, glorify thy Son that thy Son may glorify thee. Holy Spirit, do thine office and take of these things of Christ and reveal them unto us. We gather up all our prayers in that salvation through the blood of the Lamb. Amen.

PRAYER 24

'Deliver us from evil'

O God, let us not be formalists or hypocrites at this time in prayer. We feel how easy it is to bow the head and cover the face, and yet the thoughts may be all astray, and the mind may be wandering hither and thither, so that there shall be no real prayer at all. Come, Holy Spirit, help us to feel that we are in the immediate presence of God, and may this thought lead us to sincere and earnest petitioning.

There are some who know not God; God is not in all their thoughts; they make no reckoning of thee, thou glorious One, but do their business and guide their lives as if there was no God in heaven or in earth. Strike them now with a sense of thy presence. Oh! that thine eternal power might come before their thoughts, and now may they join with thy reverent people in approaching thy mercy seat.

We come for mercy, great God; it must always be our first request, for we have sinned, sinned against a just and holy law of which our conscience approves. We are evil, but thy law is holy and just and good. We have offended knowingly; we have offended again and again; after being chastened we have still offended, and even those of us who are forgiven, who through thy rich love have been once for all washed from every stain, yet we have sinned grievously; and we confess it with much shame and bitter self-reproach that we should sin against such tender love, and against the indwelling of the Holy Spirit, who is in his people; and who checks them and quickens their consciences, so that they sin against light and knowledge when they sin.

Wash us yet again. And when we ask for this washing it is not because we doubt the efficacy of former cleansing. Then we were washed in blood. Now, O Saviour, repeat upon us what thou didst to the twelve when thou didst take a towel and basin and wash their feet. And when that was done thou didst tell them that he who had been washed had no need save but to wash his feet. And after that was done he was clean every whit. Oh! let thy children be in that condition this morning - clean every whit - and may they know it; and thus being clean may they have boldness to enter into the Holy of Holies by the blood of Christ; and may they now come and stand where the cherubim once were, where the glory still shines forth. And may we before a blood-besprinkled mercy seat, ourselves washed and cleansed, pour out our prayers and praises.

As for those that never have been washed, we repeat our prayer for them. Bring them, oh! bring them at once to a sense of sin. Oh! that we might see them take their first complete washing, and may they become henceforth the blood washed and the blood redeemed consecrated ones, belonging forever unto him who has made them white through his atoning sacrifice.

And, blessed Lord, since thou dost permit thy washed ones to come close to thyself we would approach thee now with the courage which comes of faith and love, and ask of thee this thing. Help us to overcome every tendency to evil which is still within us, and enable us to wear armour of such proof that the arrows of the enemy from without may not penetrate it, that we may not be wounded again by sin. Deliver us, we pray thee, from doubts within and fears without, from depression of spirit, and from the outward assaults of the world. Make us and keep us pure within, and then let our life be conducted with such holy jealousy and watchfulness that there may be nothing about us that shall bring dishonour to thy name. May those who most carefully watch us see nothing but what shall adorn the doctrine of God our Saviour in all things.

Lord, help thy people to be right as parents. May none of us spoil our children; may there be no misconducted families to cry out against us. Help us to be right as masters; may there be no oppression, no hardness and unkindness. Help us to be right as servants; may there be no eye service, no purloining, but may there be everything that adorns the Christian character. Keep us right as citizens; may we do all we can for our country, and for the times in which we live. Keep us right, we pray thee, as citizens of the higher country; may we be living for it, to enjoy its privileges, and to bring others within its burgess-ship, that multitudes may be made citizens of Christ through our means. Lord, help us to conduct ourselves aright as church members; may we love our brethren; may we seek their good; their edification, their comfort, their health. And oh! may such of us as are called to preach have grace equal to that responsibility. Lord, make every Christian to be clear of the blood of all those round about him. We know that there are some who profess to be thy people, who do not seem to care one whit about the souls of their fellow men. God, forgive this inhumanity to men, this treason to the King of kings. Rouse the church, we pray thee, to a tenderness of heart towards those among whom we dwell.

Let all the churches feel that they are ordained to bless their neighbours. Oh! that the Christian Church in England might begin to take upon itself its true burden. Let the church in

London especially, with its mass of poverty and sin round about it, care for the people and love the people; and may all Christians bestir themselves that something may be done for the good of men, and for the glory of God. Lord, do use us for thy glory. Shine upon us, O Emmanuel, that we may reflect thy brightness; dwell in us, O Jesus, that out of us may come the power of thy life. Make thy church to work miracles because the miracle worker is in the midst of her. Oh! send us times of revival, seasons of great refreshing; and then times of aggression, when the army of the Lord of Hosts shall push its way into the very centre of the adversary, and overthrow the foe in the name of the King of kings.

Now forgive thy servants in all that has been amiss, and strengthen in thy servants all that is good and right. Sanctify us to thy service, and hold us to it. Comfort us with thy presence, elevate us into thy presence. Make us like thyself, bring us near thyself, and in all things glorify thyself in us, whether we live or die.

Bless the poor, remember the needy among thine own people; help and succour them. Bless the sick, and be very near the dying. The Lord comfort them.

Bless our country. And may thy kingdom come not here only, but in every land and nation. Lands across the flood remember with the plenitude of thy grace. Let the whole earth be filled with thy glory. We ask it for Jesus' sake. Amen.

PRAYER 25

The washing of water by the word

O Jehovah, our God, thou lovest thy people, thou hast placed all the saints in the hand of Jesus, and thou hast given Jesus to be to them a leader, a commander and a husband; and we know that thou delightest to hear us cry on the behalf of thy church for thou carest for him, and thou art ready to grant to him according to the covenant provisions which thou hast laid up in store for Christ Jesus. Therefore would we begin this prayer by entreating thee to behold and visit the vine and the vineyard which thy right hand hath planted. Look upon Zion, the city of our solemnities; look upon those whom thou hast chosen from before the foundation of the world, whom Christ hath redeemed with blood, whose hearts he has won and holds, and who are his own though they be in the world.

Holy Father, keep thy people, we beseech thee, for Jesus' sake. Though they are in the world let them not be of it, but may there be a marked distinction between them and the rest of mankind. Even as their Lord was holy, harmless and undefiled, and separate from sinners, so may it be with believers in Christ. May they follow him and may they not know the voice of strangers, but come out from the rest that they may follow him without the camp.

We cry to thee for the preservation of thy church in the world, and especially for her purity. O Father, keep us, we beseech thee with all keeping, that the evil one touch us not. We shall be tempted, but let him not prevail against us. In a thousand ways he will lay snares for our feet, but, oh! deliver us as a bird from the snare of the fowler. May the snare be broken that we may escape. Let not thy church suffer dishonour at any time, but may her garments be always white. Let not such as come in among her that are not of her utterly despoil her. O Christ, as thou didst groan concerning Judas, so may thy children cry to thee concerning any that have fallen aside into crooked ways, lest the cause of Christ in the earth should be dishonoured. O God, cover, we beseech thee, with thy feathers, all the people of Christ, and keep thy church even until he shall come who, having loved his own that were in the world, loveth them even to the end.

We would ask just now that we may be washed as to our feet; we trust thou hast bathed us once for all in the sin-removing fountain. Thou hast also washed us in the waters of regeneration and given us the renewing of our minds, through Jesus Christ; but Oh for daily cleansing. Dost thou see any fault in us? Ah! we know that thou dost. Wash us that we may be clean. Are we deficient in any virtue? Oh! supply it that we may exhibit a perfect character to the glory of him who has made us anew in Christ Jesus. Or is there something that would be good if not carried to excess? Be pleased to modify it lest one virtue should slaughter another, and we should not be the image of Christ completely.

O Lord and Master, thou didst wash thy disciples' feet of old, still be very patient towards us, very condescending towards our provoking faults, and go on with us, we pray thee, till thy great work shall be completed and we shall be brethren of the First Born, like unto him. Gracious Master, we wish to conquer self in every respect; we desire to live for the glory of God and the good of our fellow men; we would have it true of us as of our Master, 'He saved others, himself he cannot save'. Wilt thou enable us especially to overcome the body with all its affections and lusts; may the flesh be kept under; let no appetite of any kind of the grosser sort prevail against our manhood, lest we be dishonoured and unclean. And let not even the most refined power of the natural mind be permitted to come so forward as to mar the dominion of the Spirit of God within us.

Oh! help us not to be so easily moved even by pain; may we have much patience, and let not the prospect of death ever cause us any fear, but may the spirit get so much the mastery of the body that we know nothing can hurt the true man. The inner new-born cannot be smitten, nor is it to die; it is holy, incorruptible, and liveth and abideth forever in the life that is in Christ Jesus.

Oh! for a complete conquest of self. Especially render us insensible to praise, lest we be too sensitive to censure. Let us reckon that to have the approbation of God and of our own conscience is quite enough; and may we be content, gracious God, to bear the cavillings of unreasonable men; yea, and to bear the misrepresentation of our own brethren. Those that we love, if they love not us, yet may we love them none the less, and if by mistake they misjudge us, let us have no hard feelings towards them, and God grant we may never misjudge one another. Doth not our Judge stand at the bar? Oh! keep us like little children who do not know, but expect to know hereafter, and are content to believe things which they do not understand. Lord, keep us humble, dependent, yet serenely joyful. May we be calm and quiet even as a weaned child, yet may we be earnest and active.

O Saviour, make us like thyself. We wish not so much to

do as to be. If thou wilt make us to be right we shall do right. We find how often we have to put a constraint upon ourselves to be right, but, oh! that we were like thee, Jesus, so that we had but to act out ourselves, to act out perfect holiness. We shall never rest till this is the case, till thou hast made us ourselves to be inwardly holy, and then words and actions must be holy as a matter of course. Now, here we are, Lord, and we belong to thee. Oh! it is because we are thine own that we have hope. Thou wilt make us worthy of thee. Thy possession of us is our hope of perfection. Thou dost wash our feet because we are thine own. Oh! how sweet is the mercy which first took us to its heart and made us all its own and now continues to deal tenderly with us, that being Christ's own we may have that of Christ within us which all may see proves us to be Christ's own!

Now we would bring before thee all thy saints and ask thee to attend to their trials and troubles. Some we know are afflicted in person, others are afflicted in their dear friends, some are afflicted in their temporal estate and are brought into sore distress. Lord, we do not know the trials of all thy people, but thou dost, for thou art the head, and the pains of all the members are centred in thee. Help all thy people even to the end.

Now we pray thee to grant us the blessing which we have already sought, and let it come upon all the churches of our beloved country. May the Lord revive true and undefiled religion here and in all the other lands where Christ is known and preached, and let the day come when heathendom shall become converted, when the crescent of Mohammed shall wane into eternal night, and when she that sitteth on the Seven Hills and exalteth herself in the place of God shall be cast down to sink like a millstone in the flood. Let the blessed gospel of the eternal God prevail, let the whole earth be filled with his glory. Oh! that we may live to see that day.

The Lord bless our country; have pity upon it. God bless the sovereign with every mercy and blessing. Grant that there may be in thine infinite wisdom a change in the state of trade and commerce, that there may be less complaint and distress. Oh! let the people see thy hand, and understand why it is laid upon them, that they may turn from wrongdoing and seek righteousness and follow after peace. Then shall the blessing return. The Lord hear us as in secret we often cry to thee on behalf of this misled land. The Lord deliver it, and lift up the light of his countenance upon it yet again, for Jesus' sake. Amen.

PRAYER 26

Prayer answered and unanswered

God of Israel, God of Jesus Christ, our God forever and ever! Help us now by the sacred Spirit to approach thee aright with deepest reverence, but not with servile fear; with holiest boldness, but not with presumption. Teach us as children to speak to the Father, and yet as creatures to bow before our Maker.

Our Father, we would first ask thee whether thou hast ought against us as thy children? Have we been asking somewhat of thee amiss, and hast thou given us that which we have sought? We are not conscious of it, but it may be so, and now we are brought as an answer to our presumptuous prayers into a more difficult position than the one we occupied before. Now it may be that some creature comfort is nearer to us than our God; we had better have been without it and have dwelt in our God and have found our joy in him. But now, Lord, in these perilous circumstances give us grace that we may not turn away from thee.

If our position now be not such as thou wouldst have allotted to us had we been wiser, yet nevertheless grant that we may be taught to behave ourselves aright even now lest the mercies thou hast given should become a cause of stumbling, and the obtaining of our hearts' desire should become a temptation to us. Rather do we feel inclined to bless thee for the many occasions in which thou hast not answered our prayer, for thou hast said that we did ask amiss and therefore we could not have, and we desire to register this prayer with thee that whensoever we do ask amiss, thou wouldst in great wisdom and love be pleased to refuse us.

O Lord, if we at any time press our suit without a sufficiency of resignation do not regard us, we pray thee, and though we cry unto thee day and night concerning anything, yet if thou seest that herein we err, regard not the voice of our cry, we pray thee. It is our hearts' desire now, in our coolest moments, that this prayer of ours might stand on record as long as we live, not as I will, but as thou wilt.

But, O Lord, in looking back we are obliged to remember with the greatest gratitude the many occasions in which thou hast heard our cry. We have been brought into deep distress, and our heart has sunk within us, and then have we cried to thee and thou hast never refused to hear us. The prayers of our lusts thou hast rejected, but the prayers of our necessities thou hast granted. Not one good thing hath failed of all that thou hast promised.

Thou hast given to us exceeding abundantly above what we asked or even thought, for there was a day when our present condition would have been regarded as much too high for us ever to reach, and in looking back we are surprised that those who did lie among the pots of Egypt should now sit every man under his vine and fig-tree; that those who wandered in the wilderness in a solitary way should now find a city to dwell in; that we who were prodigals in rags should now be children in the Father's bosom; that we who were companions of swine should now be made heirs of God and joint heirs with Christ. Oh! what encouragement we have to pray to such a prayer-hearing God who far exceeds the request of his children.

Blessed be the name of the Lord forever, our inmost heart is saying. Amen, blessed be his name. If it were only for answered prayer or even for some unanswered prayers we would continue to praise and bless thee as long as we have any being.

And now, Lord, listen to the voice of thy children's cry. Wherever there is a sincere heart seeking for greater holiness answer thou that request, or wherever there is a broken spirit seeking for reconciliation with thyself be pleased to answer it now. Thou knowest where there is prayer, though it be unuttered, and even the lips do not move. Oh! hear the publican who dares not lift his eye to heaven. Hear him while he cries, 'God be merciful to me a sinner'. Hear such as seem to themselves to be appointed unto death. Let the sighing of the prisoner come before thee! Oh! that thou wouldst grant peace and rest to every troubled spirit all over the world who now desires to turn his face to the cross and to see God in Christ Jesus.

O Lord, if there are any of thy servants exercised about the cases of others we would thank thee for them. Raise up in the church many intercessors who shall plead for the prosperity of Zion, and give thee no rest till thou establish her and make her a joy in the land.

Oh! there are some of us that cried to thee about our country. Thou knowest how in secret we groaned and sighed over evil times, and thou hast begun to hear us already, for which we desire to praise and bless thy name. But we would not cease to pray for this land that thou wouldst roll away from it all its sin, that thou wouldst deliver it from the curse of drunkenness, rescue it from infidelity, from popery, from ritualism, from rationalism and every form of evil, that this land might become a holy land.

O Lord, bring the multitudes of the working men to listen to the gospel. Break in, we pray thee, upon their stolid indifference. Lord, give them a love of thy house, a desire to hear thy gospel. And then wilt thou look upon the poor rich who so many of them know nothing about thee and are worshipping their own wealth. The Lord grant that the many for whom there are no special gospel services, but who are wrapped up in self-righteousness, may be brought to hear the gospel of Jesus that they also, as well as the poor, may be brought to Christ.

God bless this land with more of gospel light, and with more of gospel life and love. Thou wilt hear us, O Lord.

Then would we pray for our children, that they might be saved. Some of us can no longer pray for our children's conversation, our prayers are heard already. But there are others who have children who vex them and grieve their hearts. O God, save sons and daughters of godly people. Let them not have to sigh over their children as Eli did and as Samuel did, and may they see their sons and daughters become the children of the living God. We would pray for our servants, for our neighbours, for our kinsfolk of near or far degree, that all might be brought to Jesus. Do thou this, O God, of thine infinite mercy.

And as we are now making intercession we would, according to thy Word , pray for all kings, such as are in authority, that we may lead quiet and peaceable lives. We pray for all nations also. O Lord, bless and remember the lands that sit in darkness, and let them see a great light, and may missionary enterprise be abundantly successful. And let the favoured nations where our God is known, especially this land and the land across the mighty ocean that love the same Saviour and speak the same tongue, be always favoured with the divine presence and with abundant prosperity and blessing.

O Lord, thou hast chosen this race and favoured it and multiplied it on the face of the earth, and whereas with this staff it crossed this Jordan it hath now become two great nations. Lord, be pleased to bless the whole of the race and those absorbed into it, and then all other races, that in us may be fulfilled the blessing of Abraham, 'I will bless you and ye shall be a blessing'.

And now, Father, glorify thy Son! In scattering pardons through his precious blood glorify thy Son! In sending forth the eternal Spirit to convince men and bring them to his feet, Father, glorify thy Son! In enriching thy saints with gifts and graces, and building them up into his image, Father, glorify thy Son! In the gathering together of the whole company of his elect and in the hastening of his kingdom and his coming, Father, glorify thy Son! Beyond this prayer we cannot go: 'Glorify thy Son that thy Son also may glorify thee', and unto Father, Son and Holy Spirit be glory forever and ever. Amen.

PRAYER MEETINGS - AS THEY WERE AND AS THEY SHOULD BE

PRAYER MEETINGS -
AS THEY WERE AND AS THEY SHOULD BE

Among the faults, which have largely disappeared from prayer-meetings as they used to be conducted in my early days, these were the principal ones.

First, the excessive length of the prayers.
A brother would fix himself against the table-pew, and pray for twenty minutes or half-an-hour, and then conclude by asking forgiveness for his *shortcomings* - a petition which was hardly sanctioned by those who had undergone the penance of endeavouring to join in his long-winded discourse. A good cure for this evil is for the minister judiciously to admonish the brother to study brevity; and if this avail not, to job his elbow when the people are getting weary. This fault, which is the ruin of all fervency, ought to be extirpated by all means, even at the expense of the personal feelings of the offender.

Cant phrases were another evil.
'*We would not rush into thy presence as the unthinking (!) horse into the battle.*' As if horses ever did think, and as if it were not better to exhibit the spirit and energy of the horse rather than the sluggishness and stupidity of the ass. As the verse from which we imagine this fine sentence to be derived has more to do with sinning than with praying, we are glad that the phrase is on its last legs. '*Go from heart to heart as oil from vessel to vessel.*' This is probably a quotation from the nursery

romance of *Ali Baba and the Forty Thieves*, but as destitute of sense, scripture and poetry as ever sentence could be conceived to be. We are not aware that oil runs from one vessel to another in any very mysterious or wonderful manner; it is true it is rather slow in coming out, and is therefore an apt symbol of some people's earnestness; but surely it would be better to have the grace direct from Heaven than to have it out of another vessel - a Popish idea which the metaphor seems to insinuate, if indeed it has any meaning at all.

A very favourite description of the suppliant was, '*Thy poor unworthy dust*' - an epithet generally applied to themselves by the proudest men in the congregation, and not seldom by the most monied and grovelling, in which case the last two words are not so very inappropriate. We have heard of a good man who, in pleading for his children and grandchildren, was so completely beclouded in the blinding influence of this expression, that he exclaimed, 'Lord, save thy dust, and thy dust's dust, and thy dust's dust's dust!' When Abraham said, 'I have taken upon me to speak to the Lord, which am but dust and ashes,' the utterance was forcible and deeply expressive; but in its misquoted, perverted, and abused form, the sooner it is consigned to its own element, the better.

Very many other perversions of scripture, uncouth similes, and ridiculous metaphors will recall themselves to the reader; we have neither time nor patience to recapitulate them; they are a sort of spiritual slang, the offspring of unholy ignorance, unmanly imitation, or graceless hypocrisy; they are at once a dishonour to those who constantly repeat them, and an intolerable nuisance to those whose ears are jaded with them. They have had the most baneful effects upon our prayer-meetings, and we rejoice to assist in bringing them to their deserved and ignoble end.

Another evil was, mistaking preaching for prayer.
The friends who were reputed to be 'gifted' indulged themselves in public prayer with a review of their own experience, a recapitulation of their creed, an occasional running commentary upon a chapter or Psalm, or even a criticism upon the Pastor and his sermons. It was too often quite forgotten that the brother was addressing the Divine Majesty, before whose wisdom a display of our knowledge is impertinence, and before whose glory an attempt at swelling words and pompous periods is little short of profanity; the harangue was evidently intended for man rather than God, and on some occasions did not contain a single petition from beginning to end. We hope that good men are leaving this unhallowed practice, and are beginning to see that sermons and doctrinal disquisitions are miserable substitutes for earnest wrestling prayers, when our place is at the mercy-seat, and our engagement is intercession with the Most High.

Monotonous repetition frequently occurred, and is not yet extinct.
Christian men, who object to forms of prayer, will nevertheless use the same words, the same sentences, the identical address at the commencement, and the exact ascriptions at the conclusion. We have known some brethren's prayers by heart, so that we could calculate within a few seconds when they would conclude. Now this cometh of evil. All that can be said against the prayers of the Church of England, which were many of them composed by eminent Christians, and are, some of them, as beautiful as they are scriptural, must apply with tenfold force to those dreary compositions which have little virtue left, since their extempore character is clearly disproved. Oh, for warm hearts, burning with red-hot desires

which make a channel from the lip in glowing words; then, indeed, this complaint would never be made - 'What is the use of my going to the prayer meeting, when I know all that will be said if So-and-so is called on?' This is not an uncommon excuse for staying away: and, really, while flesh is weak, it is not so very unreasonable a plea; we have heard far worse apologies for greater offences. If our (so-called) 'praying men' drive the people away by their constant repetitions, one-half at least of the fault lies at their door.

Most of these diseases, we trust, are finding their cure; but the man would be hardy, not to say fool-hardy, who should affirm that there is now no room for further improvement. 'Advance' must still be our motto, and in the matter of the prayer meeting it will be found most suitable.

Our brethren will excuse our offering them advice, and must take it only for what it is worth; but having to superintend a large church, and to conduct a prayer meeting which scarcely ever numbers less than from a thousand to twelve hundred attendants, we will simply give our own notions as to the most efficient method of promoting and sustaining these holy gatherings.

1. Let the minister himself set a very high value upon this means of grace.

Let him frequently speak of it as being dear to his own heart; and let him prove his words by throwing all his vigour into it, being absent as seldom as possible, and doing all in his power to give an interest to the meeting. If our pastors set the ill example of coming in late, of frequently staying away, or conducting the engagements in a drowsy, formal way, we shall soon see our people despising the exercise, and forsaking the assembling of themselves together. A warm-hearted address of ten minutes, with a few lively words interposed between the prayers, will do much, with God's blessing, to foster a love for the prayer meeting.

2. Let the brethren labour after brevity.

If each person will offer the petition most laid upon his heart by the Holy Spirit, and then make room for another, the evening will be far more profitable, and the prayers incomparably more fervent than if each brother ran round the whole circle of petition without dwelling upon one point. Compare the subjects of prayer to so many nails; it will be better for a petitioner to drive one nail home with repeated blows, than to deal one ineffectual tap to them one after another. Let as many as possible take part in the utterance of the church's desires; the change of voice will prevent weariness, and the variety of subjects will excite attention. Better to have six pleading earnestly, than two drowsily; far better for the whole meeting that the many wants should be represented experimentally by many intercessors, than formally by two or three.

As a general rule, meetings in which no prayer exceeds ten minutes, and the most are under five, will exhibit the most fervour and life; in fact, length is a deathblow to earnestness, and brevity is an assistant to zeal. When we have had ten prayers in the hour, varied with the singing of single verses, we have far oftener been in the Spirit, than when only four persons have engaged in supplication. This is an observation confirmed by the opinion of our fellow-worshippers; it might not hold good in all cases, but it is so with us, and therefore we thus witness.

3. Persuade all the brethren to pray aloud.
If the younger and less-instructed members shrink from the privilege, tell them they are not to speak to man, but to God. Assure them that it does us all good to hear their groans and ineffectual attempts at utterance. For our own part, a few breakdowns generally come very sweetly home; and, awakening our sympathies, constrain us to aid the brother by our more earnest wrestlings. It gives reality and life to the whole matter, to hear those trembling lips utter thanks for new life just received, and to hear that choking voice confessing the sin from which it has just escaped. The cries of the lambs must mingle with the bleating of the sheep, or the flock will lack much of its natural music. As Mr Beecher well says:

> Humble prayers, timid prayers, half-inaudible prayers, the utterances of uncultured lips, may cut a poor figure as lecture-room literature; but are they to be scornfully disdained? If a child may not talk at all till it can speak fluent English, will it ever learn to speak well? There should be a process of education going on continually, by which all the members of the church shall be able to contribute of their experiences and gifts; and in such a course of development, the first hesitating, stumbling, ungrammatical prayer of a confused Christian may be worth more to the church than the best prayer of the most eloquent pastor.

Every man, feeling that he is to take part in the meeting at some time or other, will become at once more interested, and from interest may advance to love. Some of those who have now the best gifts of utterance had few enough when they began.

4. Encourage the attendants to send in special requests for prayer as often as they feel constrained to do so.
These little scraps of paper, in themselves most truly prayers, may be used as kindling to the fire in the whole assembly.

5. *Suffer neither hymn, nor chapter, nor address, to supplant prayer.*
We remember hearing seven verses of a hymn, ending with 'He hates to put away,' until we lost all relish for the service, and have hardly been reconciled to the hymn ever since. Remember that we meet for prayer, and let it be prayer; and, oh, that it may be that genuine, familiar converse with God which shall drive out the formality and pomposity which so much mar our public supplications!

6. *It is not at all amiss to let two or even three competent brethren succeed each other without a pause*, but this must be done judiciously; and if one of the three should become prolix, let the pause come in as soon as he has finished.

Sing only one verse, or at the most two, between the prayers, and let those be such as shall not distract the mind from the subject by being alien from the spirit of the meeting. Why need to sing about the temptations of Satan just after an earnest prayer for the conversion of sinners; and when a brother has just had a joyous fellowship with Christ in intercession, why drag him down by singing, *'Tis a point I long to know*?

Of course, we ought to have said all manner of good things about the necessity of the Holy Spirit; but upon that matter we are all agreed, knowing right well that all must be in vain without his presence. Our object has rather been to gather out the stones from the way than to speak of that Divine life which alone can enable to run therein.